Deity of the Holy Spirit :
creation
inspiration
regeneration
conviction
baptism
sealing
sanctification

G. Raymond Carlson

SPIRITUAL
DYNAMICS

The Holy Spirit in Human Experience

Salvation
Father planned it
Son provided it
Spirit brings it

Radiant BOOKS

Gospel Publishing House/Springfield, Mo. 65802

02-0894

© 1976 by the Gospel Publishing House
Springfield, Missouri 65802. All rights reserved.
Adapted from *The Holy Spirit* by Frank M. Boyd, © 1963
by the Gospel Publishing House. Library of Congress
Catalog Card Number 76-5633. ISBN 0-88243-894-8.
Printed in the United States of America

**A teacher's guide for individual or group study with this
book** is available from the Gospel Publishing House (**order
no. 32-0168**). ISBN 0-88243-168-4

Contents

1
Who
~~What~~ Is the Holy Spirit?

Dr. Norman MacLean tells about the British minister who was examining his class at the Colinton Parish School. He had required the class to memorize The Apostles' Creed and repeat it clause by clause, each student having his own clause.

The first boy began, "I believe in God the Father Almighty, Maker of heaven and earth."

The second boy said, "I believe in Jesus Christ his only Son, our Lord."

The recitation continued until it reached the point where one of the boys said, "He ascended into heaven, and sitteth on the right hand of God the Father Almighty; from thence he shall come to judge the quick and the dead."

Then there fell a silence that indicated something had gone wrong. The silence was broken by the next boy in line who said, "Please sir, the boy who believes in the Holy Ghost is absent today."

SIMPLY ABSENT

There are many people who are absent when it comes to that part of the gospel. They are just simply absent—unaware of the person and work of the Holy Spirit.

Too many churches suffer from a lack of the presence and power of the Holy Spirit. Many have a doctrine of a Presence without a real Presence. The

5

Holy Spirit is replaced by a dependence upon ecclesiastical machinery and denominational programs.

DEMAND WITHOUT DYNAMIC

E. Stanley Jones brought it into sharp focus when he said, "We are presenting a Holy Spiritless Christianity—a demand without a dynamic." And how tragically true this is. But that's not the Biblical way. And it doesn't have to be your way. You can know the power and fullness of the Spirit personally. We need the boy who "believes in the Holy Ghost." You can be that one!

Strange, isn't it, how many ideas we get. Lots of folk are absent when it comes to matters of the Spirit. The fact that men are dominated by self doesn't seem to disturb a lot of professing Christians.

Religionists believe in the Holy Spirit, provided that He behaves properly and blesses the activities that they have arranged without His help.

Others have the idea that the Spirit-filled life is closely allied to the success motive of the human heart. Honestly now, do honor, prestige, and financial success always indicate the blessing of the Holy Spirit? Let's seek answers.

WHO IS THE HOLY SPIRIT?

The question finds its solution when we answer two other important questions. Is the Holy Spirit God? Is the Holy Spirit a Person?

Chief among the problems that concern the Holy Spirit is the denial of His deity and personality. Certain ancient sects of Christianity considered the Spirit to be a created being, making Him of necessity less than God. Some think the three Persons of the Holy Trinity are nothing more than separate modes of existence of a uni-personal God. The Spirit has also been viewed as a power or an influence emanating

6

from God. As such, He naturally would fail to possess the necessary characteristics of personality.

There are a number of reasons why the personality of the Spirit has been questioned. In contrast to the Father and the Son, the work of the Holy Spirit appears somewhat impersonal. The Spirit rarely speaks of himself but is content with the divine arrangement to occupy the background position.

THERE'S A DIFFERENCE

You may say, "I believe that He is God and that He is a Person, but what of it?" But it does make a difference. Whether the Holy Spirit is a Person and God of very God, or a power that God the Father sends into or exerts in our lives makes all the difference in the world.

If we think of the Spirit as an influence or power, we'll think of Him as a force that we are able to get hold of and use. If we think of the Spirit as the Bible presents Him, we will think of Him as a Person who is to get hold of us and use us.

Do you possess the influence or power, or does the Person possess you? It's important. If you think of the Spirit as an influence or power, no matter how divine, you'll always be thinking and striving to get more of the power.

LET HIM GET YOU

If you think of the Spirit as a Person, you'll concentrate on letting Him get more of you. It's not for you to get the Spirit to use Him, but for Him to get you and use you. It can result in either self-exaltation or self-humiliation. For you to boast about having the power can lead to feeling superior. For you to be possessed of the Spirit as He comes and makes you His temple will cause you to recognize His preeminence.

7

BELIEF MATTERS

What you believe about the Holy Spirit is important. Belief is important. Our world is in a mess because of wrong beliefs.

Belief matters! Refuse to believe the warning about a mad dog or a kicking horse, mister, and you're in trouble. You want your children to believe you about matches and hot wires, sharp knives and poisons. What they believe can mean life or death.

What we believe about God—God the Father, God the Son, and God the Holy Spirit—makes a world of difference. And the Bible gives us our answers.

IS THE HOLY SPIRIT GOD?

The Bible says that He is. In the Old Testament the Spirit is spoken of as the Lord God (Isaiah 61:1). In the New Testament Peter accuses Ananias of having lied to the Holy Spirit, which he declares is a lie to God (Acts 5:3,4). Paul also clearly enunciates the deity of the Spirit (2 Corinthians 3:17).

FORGET YOUR MATH

Concerning the Trinity—and you'll find the doctrine from Genesis to Revelation—there are some things that are hard to understand. You're going to have to forget all you've learned in school about thinking mathematically.

You see, God is not a problem in addition or division. The Holy Spirit is not one third of God. Nor is He one member of a three-man committee.

EQUAL RIGHTS

Throughout the Bible the Spirit is associated with an equality of being, position, and responsibility with the Father and the Son (1 Corinthians 12:4-6; 2 Corinthians 13:14; Matthew 28:19; Revelation 1:4). For reasons unrelated to position or ability, the Son is given second place and the Spirit the third in the order in which the title of God as a Trinity is stated in the Scriptures. But every characteristic of Deity belongs as much to the Spirit as to the Father and the Son.

Divine characteristics—theologically they're called attributes—are ascribed to the Holy Spirit. The Bible says He is eternal, everywhere-present, all-powerful, and all-knowing (Hebrews 9:14; 1 Corinthians 2:10, 11; Luke 1:35; Psalm 139:7-10).

The Spirit is linked with the Father and the Son in such passages as the baptismal formula (Matthew 28:19) and the apostolic benediction (2 Corinthians 13:14). Perhaps one of the most convincing statements in the New Testament is the one regarding the baptismal formula. There the Spirit is linked equally with the Father and the Son in the singular name of God.

FUZZY THINKING

There is some fuzzy thinking regarding the Trinity. For instance, some believe that God the Father was the manifestation of God in Old Testament days. This God became incarnate in the person of Jesus Christ, and today He appears as the Holy Spirit. But you can't eliminate either the Second or Third Person of the Godhead in either Testament.

Believing the Biblical evidence about the deity of the Spirit is vital. Unless the Spirit is truly God and absolutely equal with the Father and the Son, He can't do the specific things in our lives we are told He is to do.

The works of the Spirit declare His deity. The Bible specifically mentions creation (Genesis 1:2; Psalm 104:30), inspiration (2 Peter 1:20,21; 2 Timothy 3:16), regeneration (John 3:5,6; Titus 3:5), conviction (John 16:8-11; Genesis 6:3), baptism (1 Corinthians 12:13), sealing (Ephesians 1:13; 4:30), and sanctification (2 Thessalonians 2:13; Galatians 5:22, 23).

THE DIVINE EXECUTIVE

The Spirit is the Executive of the Godhead. He works in all spheres, physical and moral. Through the Spirit God created and preserves the universe. Through the Spirit God became incarnate in human flesh. Through the Spirit God works converting sinners and sanctifying and sustaining believers.

The Spirit proceeds from God, is sent by God, and is God's gift to us. How He can be one with God and yet distinct from the Father and the Son is one of the mysteries of the Trinity. To not believe it is to be driven to false doctrine; to understand it is to be driven to "wit's end" corner.

If the Holy Spirit is God, a logical question follows:

IS THE HOLY SPIRIT A PERSON?

Yes, the Holy Spirit is a Person. He acts as a Person. He speaks (2 Samuel 23:1,2; Acts 1:16; 28:25). He works wonders (Acts 2:4; 8:39). He commands (Acts 8:29; 10:19,20; 13:2; 16:6,7). He appoints (Acts 20:28). He wills (1 Corinthians 12:11).

The Spirit possesses sensibility as a Person. He can be grieved (Ephesians 4:30). He can be resisted (Acts 7:51). He can be blasphemed (Mark 3:29). He can be lied to (Acts 5:3). These are human responses to another person, not to a mere force.

Personal masculine pronouns are used to refer to the Spirit (John 14:17,26; 16:7-13).

To be a person one must have intellect, which is the ability to know; emotion, which is the ability to feel; and will, which is the ability to direct. These qualities mark you and me as personalties. Only persons think, speak, and will. These are the marks of God the Father and God the Son; and they are the marks of the Holy Spirit.

The intellect of the Spirit is seen in 1 Corinthians 2:10,11; His emotion is manifested in Ephesians 4:30; and His will is demonstrated in 1 Corinthians 12:11.

TITLES ... NOT NAMES

Strangely, no name is revealed in the Bible by which the Spirit may be designated. We can address the First Person as Father, the Second Person as Jesus or Christ or Lord or Saviour. But the Spirit is differentiated by titles. He is designated as the Spirit of your Father (Matthew 10:20), Spirit of God (Matthew 12:28), Spirit of the Lord (Luke 4:18), Holy Spirit (Luke 11:13), Spirit of Truth (John 14:17), Spirit of Life (Romans 8:2; Revelation 11:11), Spirit of Adoption (Romans 8:15), the Lord is that Spirit (2 Corinthians 3:17), Spirit of His Son (Galatians 4:6), Spirit of Jesus Christ (Philippians 1:19), Spirit which He hath given us (1 John 3:24), Eternal Spirit (Hebrews 9:14), the Comforter (John 15:26), the Spirit of Glory (1 Peter 4:14), and the seven Spirits (Revelation 1:4).

Why the Spirit used only descriptive titles as He authored the Word is not fully known. We do know that He never speaks of himself, but declares what is said to Him by the Son (John 16:13,14).

The Spirit executes the designs of the Father and executes the purpose of the Son. He applies the values which come to fallen man through the Son and carries them out in redeemed men. His measureless undertakings as Executive and Administrator of the divine purpose, from its beginning until its final consummation in glory, is beyond our comprehension.

The Bible plainly and explicitly shows that the Holy Spirit is God and that He is a Person. To deny Him personality is to deny the truth of the Trinity and to consign the Spirit to being merely an influence or force. But if He is more than a force, why does the Bible speak of Him in terms of

SYMBOLS

Often the Holy Spirit is referred to under the concept of power (Luke 4:14; 24:49; Acts 1:8). This does not imply that the Spirit is power; rather, that power is one of His characteristics. We must take great care to think of the Spirit as a Person. The emphasis on His power, which is right and proper, needs to be balanced by the even more important emphasis on His deity and person. Power is but one of His manifestations. To further describe the Spirit the Bible uses many symbolic terms. He is represented as

FIRE

The Spirit is the great Consumer and Refiner. His purging presence burns out dross and iniquity and brings illuminating, life-giving light. The Spirit is likened to

WIND

In the Bible the word for *wind* and the *spirit* is the same. The two concepts are not confused, but their qualities and characteristics are much alike. Invisible and yet everywhere intangible, imminent and tremendously important are the marks. The wind purifies the atmosphere, blowing away pollution, fog, and smoke. Wind speaks also of strength and force. Another symbol used to describe the Spirit is

WATER

Water is absolutely essential for physical life. A

person can live for 40 days without food, only 3 days without liquid. The Spirit is essential for spiritual life. Water cleanses; so does the Spirit. Water refreshes; so does the Spirit. Still another metaphor is

OIL

Oil is the paradoxical liquid—latent with fire, yet soothing. It speaks of power, action, and unction. It has a lubricating quality and is a soothing balm for soreness and pain, and an anointing for gladness. Yet another symbol is the

DOVE

The dove speaks of gentleness, tenderness, innocence, peace, purity, and patience.

The brooding presence, the *dove,* is the secret of Christian success. *Water* describes the irresistible power of the Spirit. *Fire* expresses the energy of God. *Wind* produces the breath in lost men and carries the fire along. *Oil* represents the lubricating, soothing, gladdening force that binds the people of God together and builds His kingdom.

CERTAIN CONCLUSIONS FOLLOW

The full Biblical evidence of the deity of the Holy Spirit is impregnable. Since the Bible sustains the deity of the Spirit certain conclusions follow. Because He is God we ought always to revere and obey Him. Because He indwells us we ought to cherish and honor Him. As our Teacher, we may depend upon Him for all spiritual knowledge. We can trust Him to supply our needs and depend upon Him for every spiritual good. Little wonder then that we burst forth in song and praise to the Blessed Trinity.

MORE THAN GUIDANCE . . . A GUIDE

On a trip to the South Pacific, my wife and I had

a beautiful experience that illustrates the personality of the Holy Spirit.

One of the places of ministry was in the Fiji Islands. We had read about this idyllic country. My brother and his wife, who are missionaries there, had outlined specific instructions. We arrived at the international airport at Nadi, passports in hand, prepared to go through all the legal red tape connected with entering a country as foreigners.

Imagine our pleasant surprise upon being met by a dear Fijian Christian who had been a guest in our home on two occasions. He had an official position at the airport. Within moments he had our baggage through customs; and, almost before we knew what had happened, we were on our way.

We came to Fiji with instructions for guidance, but we were blessed with a *guide*. Although we may have lots of guidance on our pilgrim journey, we have something better—we have a *Guide!* He is none other than the blessed person of the Holy Spirit.

2
Moving, Striving, and Dwelling in the Old Testament

Back and forth went the man with the lawn mower, leaving a wide space of velvetlike grass with every round. Stopping at the end of the yard, he noticed a slight movement on the machine between the two wheels. Getting down on his knees, he saw that the moving object was a tiny measuring worm.

He started the mower again and let the little worm measure his way here and there over the machine. To the worm, the machine was a whole world. When the man reached the other end of the lawn, the little "breath of life" was still busy at its work of measuring. Every few minutes the man looked down to make sure it had not fallen off.

When he finished his mowing and returned the mower to the shed, the measuring worm had also reached its long journey across the mower. He left it measuring the other side.

How big and interesting and mysterious the mower was to that worm. And it knew no more of the man than of the stars shining in the sky at night. The worm knew nothing of the distance covered by the machine; his world was the mower. The yard was as the universe.

WE KNOW SO LITTLE

With all of the scientific advances of our age, with

its expanded understanding of our world and the universe, we still know so little. We circle the sun once a year and never realize we have moved. Surely there is Someone who operates it all—who makes the "machine" go. That Someone is God. And that God is a Triune Being—Father, Son, and Holy Spirit.

Much concerning the Holy Spirit is discovered in the Old Testament, but as in the case of the Son, or more precisely, the doctrine of the Trinity, the more complete revelation is given in the New Testament. Though much additional material concerning the Spirit awaits the coming of the New Testament, the Old Testament leaves no vital feature undisclosed.

NO FANFARE

While several books of the Old Testament make no reference to the Spirit, His person, power, and presence are assumed. Without introduction or fanfare He is mentioned in the second verse of the opening book of the Bible.

The first book in the Bible, Genesis, is known as the "Book of Beginnings." It is also aptly described as the "seedplot" of the Bible. Every important revelation from God is found in germ form in Genesis; among these is the doctrine of the Holy Spirit.

There are only three references to the Spirit of God in Genesis. He is shown as moving "upon the face of the waters" (1:2), as striving with man (6:3), and as indwelling Joseph (41:38). As Donald Gee points out, these three "constitute a remarkably accurate and illuminating foreshadow of the work of the Holy Spirit in later human experience."

MOVING UPON THE WATERS

The Holy Spirit was the Agent in the creative works of God. "The Spirit of God moved upon the face of the waters," Genesis (1:2) declares.

For some cause not fully revealed, part of God's universe, the earth, required further attention. All was chaos, and darkness enshrouded the deep. The Spirit moved, literally "fluttered" over and hovered or brooded, upon the earth's dark and void substance.

The Bible provides us with a picture of the function of the Spirit as the life-energy of creation. Apparently the earth was moving through space without life or the necessary ingredients to sustain life; a shapeless, chaotic mass. But the Spirit was present hovering over this disorder.

ORDER OUT OF CHAOS

At a given moment, a Word proceeded from the mouth of God, and this Word brought order. The Word and the Spirit brought creation. Both the objective Word of the Lord and the subjective presence of the Holy Spirit were involved.

The Executor of the Holy Trinity carried forward the creative commands of God—"Let there be. . . ." Without the Spirit our planet earth would have continued void; but the Holy Trinity together created.

The Holy Spirit is the energizing Personality. He continues to do the will of the Godhead and provides life-giving energy to all nature. He preserves nature. "The grass withereth, the flower fadeth; because the the spirit of the Lord bloweth upon it" (Isaiah 40:7). All of the forces of nature are but evidences of the presence and power of the Spirit executing God's will in the world about us.

The Spirit is the Principle of order and life, the personal, organizing Authority in all creation. Job gives us this testimony, "The Spirit of God hath made me, and the breath of the Almighty hath given me life" (Job 33:4). The Spirit is the active Agent in man's creation and provides him with continuing life and sustenance.

The miracle of the new birth is brought about by the Spirit. "Except a man be born of water and of the Spirit, he cannot enter into the kingdom of God" (John 3:5). The Spirit again exerts life-giving energy and brings the sinner from the chaos of sinful darkness to the light and order of the kingdom of God.

THE FINAL TOUCH

At creation the One called upon to perfect the work was the Holy Spirit. The plan was to make the earth, among all God's handiwork, an example of beauty and usefulness. The purpose of Genesis 1 is to tell us that this was accomplished. What a picture of light, life, and love, with the creation of man as the climax! The Spirit is the First Cause of it all.

"STRIVING WITH" MAN

The second reference to the Spirit in Genesis (6:3) presents an entirely different picture. At creation the imagery was a bird brooding, hovering, fluttering, bringing life into existence. This second instance pictures a struggle. "My Spirit shall not always strive with man." Effort, contention, and conflict are involved.

Between the first mention of the Spirit in Genesis and the second one, man by voluntary transgression fell, and the human race came to a wretched state of depraved rebellion. God's love reached out to sinning humans, and the active power in that reach was the Spirit. He literally "strove" with them. One of His ministries is to convince men of sin (John 16:8). Down through the centuries the Holy Spirit has striven with rebellious souls, for God is not willing that any should perish.

THE LOVE OF THE SPIRIT

Have you ever thought of the love of the Spirit?

We hear sermons on the love of the Father and the Son—none too many—but we don't hear enough on the love of the Spirit. We owe salvation as much to Him as to the Father and the Son.

If it had not been for the love of the Spirit sent from the Father through the Son to search me out, to patiently woo me, following me, never taking "no" for an answer, bringing to bear on me all His love, grace, and wisdom, I would be on the road to hell, or maybe even in hell today.

HELP FOR LIFE'S GREATEST DECISION

I know of a young lady in Minnesota who was so seized of the Spirit in convicting power that she literally fainted in the service. The decision you must make about your eternal soul is your greatest in life. How grateful we should be to God for the work of the Spirit.

The Holy Spirit works with tremendous power to convict the sinner. He gently brings pressure to bear on the lost one to bring him to his senses. Thank God for the convicting power of the Spirit.

HE SPEAKS TO THE INNER EAR

The Spirit not only strives with sinners, He strives with believers, too, when they resist the will of God. The general tenor of our lives is guided by the Scriptures for they are the voice of God. All other voices must bow before the Word. The Spirit speaks to us through the Word and to our inner ear, the ear of our soul and spirit. No doubt many have heard the voice of the Spirit to their outer physical ear, but for the most part He speaks to the inner ear, directly to the soul.

HE REPROVES

Stray from the Lord's side, grow lukewarm in your

experience, fail to read His Word and pray, let your attendance slacken at His house, and the Spirit will strive. Lose your temper, gossip, and bear tales, and the Spirit will reprove.

A good friend, prominent in business circles, began to allow the affairs of life to cut in on his devotion to the Lord. Illness came, and the Spirit began to strive with him. All of those things that had seemed so necessary and important became trivial. He turned his face to God and then came healing for his body, peace in his heart, and joy in his life.

BUT . . . THERE'S AN END

The Spirit will not always strive with us. His long-suffering is amazing, but there comes an end to it. The Flood at the time of Noah is our example.

One of the unequivocal statements of the Bible is, "The wages of sin is death" (Romans 6:23). Sin can't pay off in any other way. Resist the pleadings of the Spirit and eventually payday comes.

I have stood at the bedside of men who have resisted until it was too late. Those scenes are indelibly stamped on my memory, as calloused men came to that dreadful moment and went into eternity cursing and foaming at the mouth. "My Spirit will not always strive with man"!

"DWELLING WITHIN" MAN

The third reference to the Spirit in the Book of Genesis introduces us to a vital truth. The Spirit indwells men. This is the testimony of a heathen ruler about his prime minister Joseph, a God-fearing man: "And Pharaoh said unto his servants, Can we find such a one as this is, a man in whom the Spirit of God is" (41:38).

The moment a person accepts Christ as his personal Saviour the Holy Spirit takes up residence in his heart (Romans 8:9). This brings fulfillment of God's purpose for human experience of the Holy Spirit as related to salvation. "Know ye not that your body is the temple of the Holy Ghost which is in you. . .?" (1 Corinthians 6:19). How beautiful—the Spirit no longer brooding over, no longer striving with, but abiding within, bearing witness to us that we are the children of God.

HELP FROM INSIDE

To have the indwelling Spirit is to have a Person within who knows us thoroughly. He takes charge and deals with us from the inside. Knowing everything about us, nothing escapes Him. Our sins, our fears, our tensions, our inhibitions, our struggles, our hopes, our yearnings, all are known by Him; not a thought or a feeling eludes Him.

No one but God can help us from inside, and He dwells within to do just that. He will deal adequately with sin and master it from the inside. From Him will come the strength to live a Christlike life, for in the person of His Spirit Christ himself has His home in our hearts (Ephesians 3:16,17,20; Philippians 2:13; Galatians 4:6).

EVIDENCE OF THE SUPERNATURAL

Have you noticed that Pharaoh's testimony concerning the indwelling of Joseph by the Spirit was compelled by a manifestation of the supernatural in Joseph's life? First of all, it was through his interpretation of Pharaoh's dreams and, second, by his God-given word of wisdom that directed the saving of a nation from starvation.

Powerful manifestations of the Spirit are evidences of the Holy Spirit possessing members of the body of Christ as they're filled with the Spirit. I speak here of an experience subsequent to salvation, the baptism in the Holy Spirit. The ultimate fulfillment of the purpose of the Spirit indwelling God's people, revealed in seed-form in Genesis, is the outflow of "rivers of living water" from the innermost being of those who have become the "temple of the Holy Ghost."

DOWN-TO-EARTH . . . UP-TO-DATE

Suppose I desperately need God right now. What shall I do? Leaf through a book and find comfort in what God *used* to do? Not at all!

God was down-to-earth in Jesus Christ. He's up-to-date by the Holy Spirit. He is neither a cosmic Craftsman safely tucked away in a far-off place, nor has He gone into retirement. He is *present now* and *powerful today*. Because of the Holy Spirit, what God did in Christ happens to me today. Because of the Spirit, I read of God's mighty acts as recorded in the Bible, and they come pouring into my own life. Humdrum existence is revolutionized by powerful workings of the Spirit. That's down-to-earth; that's up-to-date; it's God the Holy Spirit!

SPECIAL MINISTRIES

Great importance is placed upon the ministry of the Spirit to man in the Old Testament. Specific enablements for divine service are attributed to the Holy Spirit in numerous cases. The Spirit was the Source of wisdom, unusual physical strength, special skills, miracles, and divine revelation.

The Spirit came upon individuals for special ministries (Numbers 24:2; 1 Samuel 10:10). He came upon Gideon, literally "clothed him, embracing him like a coat of armor with the Spirit of God" to deliver Israel from the oppression of the Midianites (Judges 6:34). Other examples are given in 1 Chronicles 12:18 and 2 Chronicles 24:20.

In reference to the origin of their power, the prophets, priests, and kings of the Old Testament times declared that the Spirit came upon them, energized them, filled them, and laid hold upon them. In addition to those mentioned above there is Bezaleel, who was filled with the Spirit in "wisdom . . . understanding . . . knowledge, and in all manner of workmanship" for the purpose of constructing the tabernacle in the wilderness (Exodus 31:2).

Another vivid example is Samson, who by the Spirit's strength carried away the gates of Gaza and performed other feats requiring supernatural strength.

THEN FOR A FEW . . . NOW AVAILABLE TO ALL

The Spirit of God was experienced only by a select few in the Old Testament. Since the Day of Pentecost He can be the possession of all. As a rule, He was not the permanent possession of Old Testament persons, but came upon them for specific tasks. In the New Testament He is the permanent possession of all believers (Romans 8:14-16).

RUN-OF-THE-MILL

In the Old Testament the most spectacular evidence of the Spirit in the religious life of man is seen in the experiences of the prophets. Through them God communicated His Word (Zechariah 7:12), and to them He revealed His secrets (Amos 3:7). The Spirit was the power in which the prophet proclaimed his message (Micah 3:8). It followed naturally that the prophet was known in Israel as the man who was "full of power by the Spirit of the Lord" (Micah 3:8).

So the Spirit of the Lord came upon run-of-the-mill men, and they became men-in-motion, men with a message, men who did supernatural things.

The most important work of the Holy Spirit in the Old Testament is in relation to divine revelation and inspiration of the Scriptures. While the most explicit statements on this doctrine are found in the New Testament (2 Peter 1:21; 2 Timothy 3:16), inspiration in the Old Testament is declared by the selfsame Spirit.

David declared, "The Spirit of the Lord spake by me, and his word was in my tongue" (2 Samuel 23:2). Ezekiel recorded, "The Spirit entered into me when he [Jehovah] spake unto me" (Ezekiel 2:2). Micah rejoiced, "Truly I am full of power by the Spirit of the Lord" (Micah 3:8). Isaiah connected the words which God put in his mouth with the Spirit which came upon him (Isaiah 59:21). Such references reveal the activity of the Spirit in the inspiration of the Old Testament.

3

Dunamis in the New Testament

Have you ever really looked at the work of Christ and His followers as recorded in the Gospels? the work of the apostles and the believers as vividly portrayed in the Book of Acts? the place of the Spirit in the work of the Church as given in the Epistles? the work of the Spirit in Revelation?

Following Pentecost 3,000 converts were daily "in the temple, and breaking bread from house to house . . . with gladness and singleness of heart . . . And the Lord added to the church daily such as should be saved" (Acts 2:46,47).

A contemporary report of our times might read: "They daily worked revising and expanding the constitution and bylaws. Seven boards and ten committees were formed to plan strategy and set policies. An apostle was made chairman of each. Secretaries were chosen and minutes were kept. Commissions were established. So much time was needed for operating the machinery that there was little left for getting on with the job of reaching the lost. Not very many were saved."

ORGANIZATION IS IMPORTANT BUT . . .

Well, I believe in organization and planned effort. The Bible teaches it. God has always acted according to a divinely conceived plan. Jesus practiced it and taught His disciples accordingly. All of God's creation operates by organization. The efforts of revival in the Church would be wasted if there were no organization to conserve the results.

But the priorities are important. How much of eternity is involved in what you are doing? Does preoccupation with church work and sideline observations and interpretations of the world's need keep us from moving the ball toward the goal?

Remember that the more machinery there is, the more oil it takes to keep it all running smoothly. The oil of the Holy Spirit is essential in the operation of God's work.

ONE GREAT NEED

Dr. Jonathan Goforth was asked by Armin Gesswein, "What is the one great need of the Church today?" Without hesitation Dr. Goforth replied, "The Church does not know the Holy Ghost." Ignorance and neglect of the Holy Spirit are so prevalent that many church members would have to say with the people at Ephesus, "We have not so much as heard whether there be any Holy Ghost" (Acts 19:2).

THREENESS ... ONENESS

Human wisdom can never understand the Almighty. The unity—and the separateness—of the Father, Son, and Holy Spirit stand as an eternal paradox, defying finite comprehension. We must remember the threeness, for it signifies rich differentiation within the Godhead. We must remember the oneness, for it signifies that we deal, not with three gods, but with one God.

The discovery of the Holy Spirit is, for most Christians, an advanced step. Many people who believe in God the Creator, and in Christ the Redeemer, find the Holy Spirit vague, indefinite, and unnecessary.

Some people stop way back in the life of Christ. They accept His teachings but stop short of the Cross, with both its shame and its atoning power. They view the Resurrection with a vague kind of hope of immortality. The Ascension is really quite beyond them. And the Holy Spirit—well, that's way out there somewhere in limbo! And that's just why they think they're Christians when all they have is some kind of ethical humanism.

NOT ENOUGH

"I believe in the Holy Ghost." These words are uttered every week by hundreds of thousands. A part of the traditional Apostles' Creed, this affirmation is accepted by many liturgical church people as belief in the Third Person of the adorable Godhead. While it may attest to mental acceptance of the existence of the Third Person of the Holy Trinity, more is needed. Even the devil and his demons believe and tremble.

Our understanding of the Holy Spirit stems chiefly from the self-revelation of God found in the Bible. Human thinking may organize or systematize the facts of that revelation but it is unable to add to it. We do not learn of the Spirit from human experience, for experience needs the correction of divine revelation and must be interpreted in the light of it. The Scriptures are the only final authority.

MORE THAN BELIEF

Belief, however, must be translated into experience or it is without effect. Suppose I am struggling to swim and at the point of going under. You see my predicament and remark to your companion, "I believe that's our friend." Your companion looks and agrees, "Yes, I believe that's him." While the two of you are believing, I'm drowning. Only action based on belief is effective.

DON'T FENCE HIM IN

Much preaching and teaching about Christ misses the mark today and does him a grave disservice. When people don't go on to a vivid experience of the Holy Spirit, thus making more complete their Christian experience, they begin putting the wrong kind of emphasis upon Jesus. They box Him into a familiar and historic corner and don't let Him out of it. They say all the orthodox and correct things about Jesus in their liturgies, their hymns, and their sermons; but sometimes these do more to conceal than to reveal Him.

Read the New Testament and you'll see the Spirit at work. The message of the Apostolic Church—and for all Christians—was the Resurrection. The blaze of the risen Christ is everywhere present in the Book of Acts and the Epistles. But the Holy Spirit was also central. The Apostolic Church went beyond the dogma or instruction about the Spirit to an indubitable experience of Him.

The full manifestation of the Spirit's personality and deity, the full meaning of His equal position in the Godhead, and the clear-cut scope and objective in His work, are declared in the New Testament. You are arrested by the fact that the truth concerning the Spirit forms a major theme in almost every book in the New Testament.

Before the Day of Pentecost the Holy Spirit was omnipresent in the world; after Pentecost He was resident. This is not a new matter, for the Second Person of the Trinity was omnipresent in the world, and after 33 years of residence here in a human body He left the world, but He still retains the omnipresent Presence (Colossians 1:27; Matthew 18:20). This helps us to understand how He could always be present in the world and still be promised by Christ as the One who was to come.

CONCEIVED BY THE SPIRIT

The same Spirit who hovered over chaos in the opening verses of Genesis was present to "overshadow" the Virgin Mary in the New Testament (Luke 1:35) causing her to conceive. The birth of Jesus was supernatural. It was a creative operation of the Holy Spirit in the womb of Mary. Jesus was conceived of the Holy Spirit and born of the Virgin Mary.

Jesus Christ was not only man, He was also God. He was the God-man. He was Deity of Deity. He works in conjunction with His Father and with the Holy Spirit.

BAPTIZED IN THE SPIRIT

Jesus was baptized in the Spirit. John the Baptist's fiery preaching demanded repentance. He announced the arrival of "one mightier than I. . . , the latchet of whose shoes I am not worthy to unloose: he shall baptize you with the Holy Ghost and with fire" (Luke 3:16).

One day Jesus came to the banks of the Jordan River to be baptized. As He prayed, the heavens opened and the Holy Spirit in the form of a dove settled upon Him. Jesus became a candidate for this enduement of power for service before beginning His public ministry (Luke 3:21,22).

LED OF THE SPIRIT

Jesus was led of the Spirit. "Then Jesus, full of the Holy Spirit, left the Jordan River being urged by the Spirit out into the barren wastelands of Judea, where

Satan tempted Him for 40 days" (Luke 4:1,2, *Living Bible*).

Following the temptation in the wilderness, Jesus "went back full of and under the power of the (Holy) Spirit into Galilee" (Luke 4:14, Amplified). He knew that the Spirit of the Lord was upon Him. This is confirmed by His public reading of Isaiah 61:1, "The Spirit of the Lord is upon me, because he hath anointed me . . ." (Luke 4:18).

THROUGH THE POWER OF THE SPIRIT

When the Pharisees charged that Jesus cast out devils by the power of Satan, He answered that He cast out evil spirits by the Spirit of God, and this was the proof that the kingdom of God was come upon them.

At Cornelius' house, Peter declared "how God anointed Jesus of Nazareth with the Holy Ghost and with power: who went about doing good, and healing all that were oppressed of the devil; for God was with him" (Acts 10:38).

This life-giving, life-sustaining Spirit anointed Jesus to heal and deliver. As one writer has written, "His human spirit was so penetrated and elevated by the Spirit of God, that it lived in the eternal and invisible, and was able to endure the cross, despising the shame."

The Scriptures clearly state that the sublime and central fact of redemption, the Atonement, was wrought by Christ on the cross by the power of the Spirit: "Who through the eternal Spirit offered himself without spot to God" (Hebrews 9:14).

If it was essential for Jesus Christ, the Son of God to have the anointing of the Holy Spirit to accomplish God's will, how much more needful for us!

THE SPIRIT PROMISED

On the very night in which He was betrayed,

Jesus comforted the disciples with the promise that He would not leave them comfortless, literally *orphans,* but that He would send them the Comforter, which is the Holy Spirit. In a resurrection appearance He breathed upon the disciples and said, "Receive ye the Holy Ghost."

Just as He was about to ascend into heaven, Jesus commanded His disciples "that they should not depart from Jerusalem, but wait for the promise of the Father, which . . . ye have heard of me" (Acts 1:4).

ONLY A PROMISE

Jesus left the defeated, forlorn disciples with a promise. There was no strategy, no great organizational plan for conquering the world; only a promise. They had seen Him as the risen Christ. He had taught them about His coming kingdom. But now only a promise. Not a promise to "at this time restore again the kingdom to Israel" (Acts 1:6). No, not at all. Only to wait at a given place for the promise of the Father. Possibly that's why only 120 of the 500 obeyed. It seemed so anti-climactic.

But while Jesus did not leave them a modern organizational chart, He did not leave His followers alone and on their own. He promised them something far better than a plan and program; He promised them a Person, the Holy Spirit. The Spirit would come to live in them and equip them with the power and guidance they so desperately needed.

HE INVADES PLANET EARTH

To the 120 waiting in the Upper Room the Holy Spirit came. On the Day of Pentecost "suddenly there came a sound from heaven as of a rushing mighty wind, and it filled all the house . . . and there appeared . . . cloven tongues like as of fire, and it sat upon each of them. And they were all

31

filled with the Holy Ghost, and began to speak with other tongues, as the Spirit gave them utterance" (Acts 2:2-4).

That was a divine visitation different from all others. Many times during the centuries since man's creation God had invaded planet earth, but this was the first time that a heavenly Person came to earth to stay. Jesus had promised that the Comforter would come to "abide with you for ever" (John 14:16).

ON SCHEDULE

The Holy Spirit arrived on schedule. He filled the waiting 120, and He remains in the world. He is here! It was in the Upper Room that the Church of the Living God started its march through time. That march shall not end until Jesus comes as King of kings and Lord of lords.

Miraculously, the Holy Spirit possessed the physical being of every member of that congregation of 120. Theirs was no mere mental assent to a new doctrine. The finest minds and most brilliant orators could not explain the transcendent experience of that day. Unbelief was eclipsed by daring faith. Weak men became strong. Cowards became bold. Unlearned and ignorant men began to turn the world upside down.

HE TAKES COMMAND

The Book of the Acts of the Apostles is in the true sense the Book of the Acts of the Holy Spirit. He takes command. He tells Philip to leave Samaria and go down to Gaza and preach to the Ethiopian eunuch. He tells Peter on the housetop at Joppa to go to Caesarea and preach to a Roman soldier, the devout Cornelius, and his household. He directs Paul in his journeys and ministry, forbidding him to preach in Asia, but opening a great and effectual door for him in Europe. He gives Paul the message: "Which things also we speak, not in the words which man's wisdom teacheth, but which the Holy Ghost teacheth" (1 Corinthians 2:13).

WHAT ABOUT TODAY?

In our era of ever-expanding knowledge there's a tendency to replace the mourner's bench with the psychiatrist's couch. The preacher designs his sermon to make people "feel" good rather than "be" good. The appeal is made on the basis of ethics instead of through the power of the Spirit.

If the Holy Spirit is not allowed to actively direct the operation of the Church by controlling the lives of its members, the Church will have lost its dynamic. We have a great deal of activity, but Christian character is not manufactured by dint of human prowess. Though we may be theologically correct, what value does that have if we do not know and have the presence of the Holy Spirit in power.

Greatness is never just strength. Hitler had strength and used it to almost exterminate a race, and in the doing scared a world half to death. The greatness of our lives is not merely in a display of strength and power; it must come through the might of the Holy Spirit who also graces the lives of those who yield to Him with the rich fruits of the Spirit.

HAVE YOU RECEIVED SINCE YOU BELIEVED?

Lest any should feel that the transforming experience recorded in the Book of Acts was only for the infant Church, Peter banished such ignorance and pessimism at Pentecost with this thrilling promise, "For the promise is unto you, and to your children, and to all that are afar off, even as many as the Lord our God shall call" (Acts 2:39). That includes you!

4

Help for Believing and Behaving

Suppose you suddenly died and came face to face with God. What would you do? You'd fall down before Him, awestruck by His majesty, His might, His greatness, His reality. You'd either worship Him or cringe in utter fear. The attitude of your heart at the time of death would determine your response as you appeared before Him (Philippians 2:9-11).

Confrontation with God is inescapable. Saul of Tarsus, the young leader who had always been on top and who always was voted "most likely to succeed," fell to the dust of the Damascus road when he met God. Blinded, scared half out of his wits, he cried, "Who are you, Lord? . . . what would you have me to do?" (Acts 9:1-8, the New Berkeley Version). That was confrontation.

Remember when Peter, James, and John had toiled all night fishing and had caught nothing (Luke 5: 2-11). Jesus told them to let down their nets, and they had a fabulous catch. In the process Peter's eyes were opened to the Lord and to himself. He fell down at Jesus' knees and said in effect, "Depart from me; go away, Lord; You don't want anything to do with me. I can't be in your presence. I'm a sinful man." That was confrontation.

The Book of Revelation (6:12-17) records fearful judgments that are to come upon this earth. Men great and small who have resisted the Spirit will say to the mountains and rocks, "Fall on us, and hide us from the face of him that sitteth on the throne, and from the wrath of the Lamb: for . . . who shall be able to stand?" That will be an awesome confrontation.

YOU CAN CHOOSE

Yes, you can't avoid confrontation with God. But you have a choice as to how and when that first confrontation occurs. You can choose whether it will be redemptive or retributive. How can that be?

God the Father and God the Son have sent the Holy Spirit to represent them. While the primary ministry of the Spirit is toward believers, there is a most essential ministry which He performs toward unbelievers. Without it no one would find Christ, for none would be troubled concerning his sin and lostness.

The manner and purpose of that confrontation are emphatically and clearly stated in John's Gospel (16:7-15). The ministry of the Spirit covers a threefold sphere of activity. First, He has a specific ministry to the world; second, to the believer; and finally, in the Church.

CONVICTED

The first function of the Spirit's ministry in the world is to "reprove [convince, convict] . . . of sin." The Bible is specific to pinpoint the sin: "because they believe not on me." The great sin of humanity is not found in actions that arise from evil minds, terrible though they be. Soul-destroying sin is unbelief, the refusal to believe in Jesus as Saviour. It's not how much "bad" we have done or how much "good" we have done. Good sinners are as lost as bad sinners. Unwillingness to relate life and self to

Jesus Christ will be the condemnation, not the list of broken rules of conduct.

THE FIRST RUNG

Conviction of sin is the first rung on the ladder of salvation. If you were trying to reach the sky, it wouldn't make much difference whether you tried from the bottom of the Grand Canyon or from the top of Mt. Everest. The difference in distance would be insignificant. Our best efforts will fail. We must believe on Christ. The Spirit comes to convince us of our sin and our inability to get rid of it. The great sin is that "they believe not in me."

The debate about "new morality," situation ethics, nonethics, and the whole bag aimed at the so-called "religious establishment" are all circumventions and diversionary. The Spirit comes to smash all that; He presents Christ. Unless we believe in the substitutionary work of Christ, we don't have a chance, not a prayer.

Confrontation with the Holy Spirit on this score is far from pleasant; it may seem hard, but there's no future without it.

CONVINCED

The second part of the Spirit's ministry to the world is to "convince" of righteousness. When His first work is done, the approach of the Spirit shifts quickly. The dark shadows of night are driven away by the bright rays of morning sun. The gloom of conviction of sin turns to hope. There is deliverance from sordid sin. Righteousness is available. It's not a matter of doing this or that good; human effort has nothing to do with it.

Righteousness is provided by Christ. By His holy life He manifested the righteousness of God which was His by inherent deity. In His sacrificial death He secured that righteousness for the believer (2 Corinthians 5:21). The giving of the Holy Spirit on the Day of Pentecost was a witness to the whole world of the validity of the Atonement and of the righteousness of Christ.

That's the second work of the Holy Spirit, to convince you of righteousness. Once you've confessed your sin and accepted Christ into your heart, the Spirit tells you on the basis of God's Word that you are righteous in God's sight.

JUDGED AT CALVARY

The final aspect of the Spirit's ministry in the world is to "convict" of judgment. No one escapes the judgment of God. This is not, however, as supposed by many, judgment to come. It concerns the fact that "the prince of this world is judged" (John 16:11). Satan was judged at Calvary. His hold over us is broken. His power over us has been destroyed. This is the message that the Spirit brings to us. Faith, appropriating this truth, brings salvation.

CAUTERIZED . . . HEALED

The second sphere of activity in the ministry of the Spirit is in the realm of the believer's life. This involves regeneration, equipping with power for service, guidance and instruction, and the impartation of spiritual gifts.

The Spirit comes to convict. He burns and cauterizes, but then He heals and regenerates.

Sin pulls us down to the animal plane, searing the conscience, blinding the reason, and paralyzing the will. The way back to God is neither a moral nor an intellectual way. We are brought back through conversion, otherwise known as the "new birth."

The regenerating ministry of the Holy Spirit involves the communication of the divine nature to us. Regeneration is not our natural life carried to its highest point of attainment, but the divine life brought down to its lowest point of condescension, even to the heart of fallen man.

WHO NEEDS SALVATION?

Most men agree that the extremely wicked need God's salvation. The immoral, irreverent, and intemperate need to be born again. But Jesus said, "Ye must be born again" (John 3:7) to a religious leader.

It's difficult to admit our weakness and inability to refine our character to meet God's standards. It's even more difficult to admit as Paul did, "For I know that in me (that is, in my flesh,) dwelleth no good thing" (Romans 7:18).

WHAT'S THE ANSWER?

We need more than creed, more than ritual, more than reformation; we need transformation. It's not what we do for religion or in the name of religion, but what Christ does for us. It's not baptism or submission to ordinances; it's not church membership.

We need the new birth. From the divine side, this change of heart is called regeneration; from the human side it is called conversion. The new birth comes from above. It's a spiritual birth, an absolute change, a new creation (2 Corinthians 5:17).

The atoning work of Christ is the ground of our salvation, and the Word of God is an instrument of regeneration (James 1:18; 1 Peter 1:23; John 5:24; Romans 10:17).

The Holy Spirit is the active Agent working with the Word of God and the blood of Christ to perform the will of God. The work of the Spirit is essential in regeneration (Romans 8:9). Paul refers to the new birth as an experience of receiving divine life, the "renewing of the Holy Ghost" (Titus 3:5).

Regeneration is the inward moving of life, the very breath of God. This is one of the major ministries of the Spirit. His work is incomprehensibly in the act of faith in Christ.

GOD PROVIDES ... WE ACT

Two great facts must be kept in mind regarding regeneration. The first is the efficiency of God; the other is the activity of man. We must take the following steps: (1) acknowledge sin (Romans 3:23; 6:23; Ezekiel 18:4; Luke 18:13); (2) repent of sin (Luke 13:3; Acts 3:19; 2 Corinthians 7:10); (3) confess sin (Psalm 32:5; 1 John 1:8); (4) forsake sin (Isaiah 55:7); (5) believe the gospel (Romans 10:9); (6) accept the Lord Jesus Christ (John 1:12).

When we take these steps, something marvelous and mysterious transpires. It is beyond human observation. Nicodemus wanted to know the "how" of regeneration (John 3:4). Jesus answered, "Marvel not. . . ." We might not be able to explain the "how," but we should know "when" the new birth took place.

THE MYSTERY OF LIFE

Physical birth is a mystery. Where and how does the "spirit" come? There's a vast difference between a stillborn child and a living one. One has abundant evidence of life; the other has none. Even so, the work of the Holy Spirit in the new birth is shrouded in mystery.

We can't account for the influence or direction of the wind. Its movements are real to us but mysterious. We can't change its course or velocity for it's controlled by a Higher Power. The wind is invisible, secret, incomprehensible; we hear its sound, feel its force, observe its work, see its effects.

That's like the work of the Spirit in regeneration (John 3:8). We "hear the sound" and then know that the breath of God has blown upon a human soul. The force is seen in the direct change in that person's life. While the origin of life may be mysterious, there is no possibility of denying the manifestation of life.

LOTS OF MYSTERIES

Mysterious? Yes. Hard to understand? Yes. But there's mystery connected to the common things of life. The same kind of forage turns into bristles for pigs, hair for cattle, wool for sheep, and feathers for chickens. Can you explain how a small black seed germinates and produces a radish with a white body, red skin, and green stem? We may not understand all the facts, yet we enjoy the benefits. Don't be bothered by the mysteries of the transformation from death unto life through the new birth.

The impartation of the Holy Spirit in the new birth and the baptism in the Spirit are two separate and distinct experiences. They should never be identified as one and the same. An entire chapter will be devoted to the baptism in the Holy Spirit.

SOMETHING FURTHER

But there is a further work of the Holy Spirit which is distinct and separate from both the new birth and the baptism in the Spirit. This is sanctification, a process which separates the sinner from the secular and sinful, and sets him apart for sacred purposes. This inward cleansing and setting apart is by the desire of the believer, and is the work of God by the Holy Spirit on the ground of the atoning work of Christ (Romans 6:1-23).

To put it simply, sanctification means holiness

40

(2 Corinthians 7:1; 1 Thessalonians 4:7; 1 Peter 1:15,16). Two great truths are involved. The first is consecration or a true relationship to God, which is separation from sin and unto God.

The second truth in sanctification is purification, or a true condition before God. The presence of the Spirit will purify our thoughts, our desires, and our actions (2 Timothy 2:21; 1 John 1:7).

IN A NUTSHELL

Our sanctification is the *purpose* of the Father (1 Thessalonians 4:3); the *purchase* of the Son (Hebrews 10:10); by the *power* of the Spirit (Romans 8:1,2); and by the *pages* of the Scriptures (John 15:3; 17:17). Let me quickly say that, while the word *pages* is used for the purpose of alliteration, the power is not in the paper and ink; it's in the inspired, inerrant, infallible, authoritative Word of God.

Christ is our sanctification (1 Corinthians 1:30); the Holy Spirit is the Sanctifier (Romans 8); and we are the sanctified.

THE SECRET

Sanctification is not suppression; it is not a matter of struggling internally to maintain outward composure. Neither is sanctification eradication (1 John 1:8). Sin is not dead, but the Christian can be dead to sin.

The Spirit comes to give the law of life over the law of sin and death. It's not constant suppression but positive counteraction: "Yield yourselves unto God" (Romans 6:13). It's not by human willpower. Willpower is weak power.

ON MASTERS AND SERVANTS

All of us have a master. Some would claim to have no master. They say they are free and servants to none. But they're wrong, absolutely wrong. You have your master, and you can choose who it will be. It's "to whom ye yield yourselves servants to obey, . . . whether of sin unto death, or of obedience unto righteousness" (Romans 6:16).

But then, how can I become the servant of righteousness? The answer is found in Ephesians 2:8-10. I must be a person of faith. And there is more: I need to have outside help. That help is found in the blessed Holy Spirit; I must walk after the Spirit.

Through union with the risen, glorified Saviour, a new power, the Holy Spirit, enters your nature to subdue sin. Through the Spirit, the righteousness which the Law required is fulfilled *in* you, not *by* you.

HALLMARKS

In Romans 8 the Spirit-controlled life is shown to be marked by: (1) spiritual harmony—"life and peace" (v. 6); (2) spiritual victory—"body is dead . . . but the Spirit is life" (v. 10); (3) spiritual mastery—"led by the Spirit" (v. 14); (4) spiritual certainty (vv. 15-39).

The Holy Spirit is mentioned about 25 times in Romans 8. The chapter begins with "no condemnation" and ends with "no separation," and in between there is "no defeat."

BELIEVE AND BEHAVE

Believe and behave! That's your responsibility. Believing brings you into fellowship with God. Behaving gives evidence that you have fellowship with God. When you believe, you enter the "straight gate"; when you behave, you walk in the "narrow way." According to Billy Graham, "A Christian ought to live so that he'd not be afraid to sell the family parrot to the town gossip!"

5

The Holy Helper

The car is new. The gas tank is full. The key is in the ignition. Seat belts are fastened. Driver's training classroom work is over. The instructor is in the right-hand seat. Susan is ready for the big moment. She slides in behind the wheel, turns the key, the motor purrs beautifully.

Shifting into drive, Susan starts down the street. All goes great until she gets into a snarl of traffic. Horns honk; tempers flare. No one pays attention to the "Driver Education" tag. Seemingly all they notice is the novice at the wheel. What can she do? Where can she turn?

Like a flash she follows impulse, jumps from the car, and runs to a nearby phone booth. Getting mother on the line, Susan cries, "Mom, what can I do? I'm scared. Traffic is so heavy. Please help me."

Mother's assuring voice helps. "What about your teacher? Isn't he with you? He knows what to do." Susan answers, "Right, Mom, I never thought of that."

Crazy illustration, isn't it? Well, that's no more preposterous than the way a lot of us act in the traffic jams of life. We forget that the heavenly Guide is right there. He's not only the Teacher; He's right at our side, available to help us.

Life is filled with difficulties. So often we don't know where to turn, and we feel like "jumping ship." But God has given us a great Helper to take the place of the visible presence of Christ. Moffatt's translation of John 14:16 reads: "I will ask the Father to give you another Helper to be with you for ever."

TWO THINGS ARE PLAIN

Two things are very plain to me. First, I need divine help to live the life that pleases God. Second, I can have all the help I need.

The first is demonstrated in experience. The other day a friend said, "A fellow needs to be made of steel to survive in days like these." But who has that quality? We do need help. Like Peter we cry, "Lord, save me."

The second is the crystal-clear promise made by Jesus. We can have all the help we need. We not only can have help, we can have the Helper himself. How does He help? Paul writes, "The Spirit . . . helpeth our infirmities" (Romans 8:26).

SPIRITUAL AIRLIFT

Several years ago Berlin was in real trouble. The Russians, as a part of their cold war strategy, cut off all food and fuel going into the city. Their objective was to starve and freeze the Berliners into submission, and to cause the Allies, who were occupying the city, to withdraw. The roads to the city were closed, and the cause of the West looked bleak. But the ingenuity and courage of the Allies hadn't been reckoned with. The Berlin airlift brought supplies from the skies. The Berliners did not starve, nor did they freeze. Neither did they surrender!

Sometimes we, like the Berliners, find ourselves

hopelessly surrounded. Defeat seems certain. But then the Holy Helper establishes His spiritual airlift and brings His limitless supply of measureless power. How can we fail?

The King James Version reads, "I will pray the Father, and he shall give you another Comforter" (John 14:16). Notice that word "another." It indicates that someone else had been a Comforter ahead of the promised Holy Spirit. Who was this? None other than Jesus himself.

The word *comforter* is translated from the Greek *parakletos* which means an intercessor, consoler, advocate, comforter, one appointed to accompany us and help us. In 1 John 2:1 the same word is translated *Advocate,* speaking of Jesus. So there are two Comforters: the Lord Jesus, who left the earth and returned to the Father, and the Holy Spirit, whom Christ sent down to earth from the Father.

EXACTLY LIKE ME

Jesus was telling the disciples, "I am not sending you Someone who is different from Me, Someone whom you do not know, Someone of whom you need to be afraid. I am sending Someone who is exactly like Me. When He comes to you, you will think of Me."

In His bodily character Jesus was limited to one place at a time. His ministry was localized during His earthly advent. What He had been to the Twelve, to those He could reach, the Holy Spirit was to become to the universal Church. That's why it was expedient for Him to return to the Father so that He could send the Comforter (John 16:7).

Jesus had helped them with their problems of sin, physical infirmities, finances, and a hundred other burdens, but they had depended upon His physical presence. Notice that Mary and Martha didn't know

45

the comfort of Jesus' power over sickness and death until He showed himself visibly.

When Jesus said that He would send another Comforter, He said that this One would perform all the things that He had done for them. Whereas Jesus' body of flesh could be only in one place, the Holy Spirit embraces the entire Church. He does all that Jesus could do by His bodily presence as the Comforter. He makes Christ's presence real to us.

WHO FALLS DOWN BESIDE US

Robert C. Cunningham shares the story of a missionary working among the Karre people in Africa. She was grasping for the right word to translate the word *Comforter*. She asked some of the leading Christians for help, explaining the way the Spirit encourages, exhorts, protects, helps, strengthens, comforts, and guides us. "Isn't there some word in your language that has this meaning?" she asked.

Finally one of them said, "If someone would do all that for us, we would say, 'He's the one who falls down beside us.'" He explained that their porters would travel great distances carrying heavy loads on their heads. At times they would collapse along the trail because of sickness or sheer exhaustion. A porter might lie there all night in danger of being killed by wild animals. However, someone might come along the trail in time to save him. He would stoop down, pick up the porter, and carry him to safety. Such a friend would be called "the one who falls down beside us."

The missionary now had what she needed. She used it to translate the word *Comforter*, for that aptly describes the Spirit's work.

AT THE END OF THE ROPE

You come to the dreaded moment. You're at the

end of the rope. Your emotions overwhelm you, be it from loneliness, failure, fear, tragedy, or sorrow, and it all seems beyond your ability to see through. The onslaught of these plaguing forces is so massive and brutal, but the Holy Helper is there.

He's always in the background, never speaking of himself (John 16:13). He performs secret service on your behalf efficiently and lovingly. He seeks to be a gracious, willing Guest in your heart. Your job is to cultivate a sensitive intimacy with Him. Let us listen to Him, to His promptings, pleadings, and wooings. Let us consult Him in all the changing scenes of changing days. Above all, let us greedily take the gifts of grace and enduement which He offers.

STRENGTHENING AND DEFENDING

Weymouth's rendering of John 14:16 reads, "And I will ask the Father, and He will give you another Advocate to be for ever with you—the Spirit of truth." Weymouth translates the Greek, employing the same word that the King James Version uses in 1 John 2:1, where it speaks of the present ministry of Christ at the right hand of the Father as an Advocate.

Paraclete is the Greek term; *Advocate* is the Latin term. This latter term bears the meaning of a counsel who pleads, convinces, and convicts in a great controversy; who strengthens on the one hand, and defends on the other. He alone is adequate to meet formidable attacks.

Just as it was expedient that Christ's advocacy should be transferred to the heavenly sphere, so it was equally expedient that the Holy Spirit should be sent not merely to be with them, but to be with them as the "other Advocate."

Although the ministries of the Holy Spirit are varied, none of them are to be ignored or neglected. Another of His wonderful ministries is that of

Because we have inherited a fallen nature from Adam, it is not natural for us to know and discern the will of God. The saints of the Old Testament repeatedly made known their longing to know God's will (Jeremiah 10:23,24; Psalm 31:3).

With the added revelation in the New Testament of the ministries of the Spirit, we see His leadings in several ways. First, we discover that Jesus himself relied on the leading of the Spirit (Matthew 4:1). The historian Luke explicitly said that it was the leading of the Spirit which inaugurated the great missionary enterprise to the Gentiles (Acts 13:1-3).

Although it is generally known that the gospel came to Europe because of Paul's Macedonian call (Acts 16:6-10), we don't often call attention to the restricting and restraining work of the Spirit in that instance. The ASV reads, ". . . having been forbidden of the Holy Spirit to speak the word in Asia . . . they assayed to go into Bithynia; and the Spirit of Jesus suffered them not . . . concluding that God had called us to preach the gospel [in Europe]."

OBEY HIS PROMPTINGS

How important to obey the promptings of the Spirit. Never will I forget a day when such a prompting came. Seemingly a hundred things were pressing upon me, demanding attention. I became impressed to drop it all and make a trip to a neighboring state to call on some friends.

The husband was not a Christian. We had a warm friendship, but he was quite opposed to the Pentecostal message, the message that is such a vital part of my preaching.

Arriving at their home, my wife and I were welcomed by the husband with these words, "How good to see you. We desperately need help. Marie is very ill. Come in." We went into the bedroom, and there the three of us—the unsaved husband, my wife, and I—knelt by his wife's bed in prayer. God touched her. Today the husband is in heaven with the Saviour he had turned aside for over 80 years of his life.

Oh to listen to the promptings of the Spirit!

YOU DON'T CARRY THE HOLY SPIRIT AROUND IN YOUR POCKET OR STRUNG ON A KEY CHAIN

He's more than a last resort to be used in case of emergency. We don't possess Him to be handed out like a meal ticket. We've got to let Him possess us and use us. It's not a mechanical matter.

On the divine side, "It is God who worketh in you both to will and to work, for his good pleasure" (Philippians 2:13, ASV). On the human side, we must present our "bodies a living sacrifice, holy, acceptable to God, which is [our] spiritual service. And be not fashioned according to this world: but be ye transformed by the renewing of your mind, that ye may prove what is the good and acceptable and perfect will of God" (Romans 12:1,2, ASV).

God has chosen to lead His people through the guidance of the Spirit (Romans 8:14; Galatians 5:18). In a day when so much stress is placed upon guidance and counseling vocationally, educationally, and mentally, it's sad to see how many children of God fail to avail themselves of the unerring guidance of the Spirit of God.

ANCHOR TO SCRIPTURE

The Holy Spirit uses the Word of God, the written revealed will of God. His promptings will never violate the Scriptures for He is the Author (2 Peter 1:21); but it is important to heed His promptings. One night I was about to introduce the evening

49

...er in our service. While seated behind the pul-
..., I had a strange experience. The Spirit spoke to
me, not audibly, but in a very real way. "You're going to have a funeral, and you're to use John 11:25 as
your text." The impression was very strong and kept
repeating itself. Now, I knew of no one in the area of
my pastoral responsibility who was ill at the time, to
say nothing of anyone dying. At that moment I noticed a lady stepping into the sanctuary. She spoke
briefly to my wife who was seated at the back. Shortly my wife beckoned to me; and, after presenting the
speaker, I slipped out a side door to get the message.
The lady requested that I come immediately to a rest
home to see her aged father who was extremely ill.
I went and had the joy of leading him to the Saviour
and returned to the service before the sermon was
concluded.

The next morning the lady was at our house to tell
us her father had died minutes after I left him. Then
she said, "I'd like you to conduct the funeral. Now I
know I shouldn't tell you what to take as a text, but
could you use John 11:25, 'I am the resurrection, and
the life: he that believeth in me, though he were
dead, yet shall he live'?" And that's the story of my
first funeral service.

THE DIVINE INFORMANT

Although Jesus had been in closest fellowship with
His disciples for those incomparable years of ministry, He uttered some amazing words before going to
Calvary. He said, "I have yet many things to say unto
you, but . . . the Spirit of truth . . . will guide you
into all truth . . . show you things to come . . . shall
glorify me . . . shall take of mine, and shall show it
unto you" (John 16:12-15).

The Holy Spirit comes as the divine Informant. He
alone can discern and impart spiritual truth, for He

is the Spirit of Truth. There is a stratum of knowledge to be gained in the material-physical realm, but there is a higher level of knowledge that can only be imparted by the Spirit (1 Corinthians 2:10-13).

This knowledge is not attained through education. As one has said, "You can pile up your training and add your degrees until finally you may totter with a cane across the last academic platform of your life," but that doesn't necessarily assure you of spiritual knowledge. There is certain knowledge that comes only through the ministry of the Spirit through God's Word. That is knowledge *of* the Spirit, and it is given *by* the Spirit.

Such knowledge comes through knowing not just about a Person, but to know Him. And there's a vast difference (Philippians 3:10).

The Holy Spirit reveals the things of God (1 Corinthians 2:10-13), and the things of Christ (John 16:14). He gives insight concerning the future (Luke 2:26; John 16:13; Acts 21:11). He helps recall the words of Christ (John 14:26), and provides answers for persecuted believers (Mark 13:11; Luke 12:12). The Spirit guides into all truth (John 14:17; 16:13). He provides the word of wisdom or of knowledge as needed (1 Corinthians 12:8), and guides the decisions of the Church (Acts 15:28). He leads in the way of godliness (Isaiah 30:21; Ezekiel 36:27).

THE DIVINE TRANSFORMER

The demands of God on the Christian are rather rigid. They are too high for the natural man to achieve. Natural ability and human genius are inadequate, but those demands are possible through the aid of the Holy Helper. He makes intercession for us according to the will of God, and transforms us to conform to the image of Christ.

The Holy Helper is:

The stamina of our spiritual life (Romans 8:2).

The source of our power (Acts 1:8).

The spring of our joy (John 15:11; Romans 14:17; Ephesians 5:18,19).

The secret of our knowledge (1 Corinthians 2:10).

The seal of our assurance (Ephesians 4:30).

Note the additional comments in Ephesians regarding the Spirit.

Through the Spirit we have access to the Father (2:18), and through Him we are "builded together for an habitation of God" (2:22). We are strengthened with might by the Spirit (3:16). We are to maintain the unity of the Spirit (4:3), to remain filled with the Spirit (5:18), and finally, to pray in the Spirit (6:18).

Make much, make everything of the ministries of the Spirit of God *to* and *in* and *through* you.

6
Filled With the Spirit

A radio preacher tells this story. "A seminary professor, in preaching on the Holy Spirit, used the following illustration. He said, 'If the President of the United States should announce that he is coming to your home, would you give him the poorest room in the house or the best room?' He went on to elaborate how you would clean the best room and put on fresh linens, get a bouquet of flowers, and have a real welcome.

"That evening we were under the trees, and he made a mistake. He said to me, 'How did you like my message?' I have never dared ask that question because, as sure as I do, someone is going to tell me the truth, and it is bound to be frustrating. But I replied, 'You asked me honestly, and I will tell you honestly. I do not think you went far enough. I do not think that the filling with the Holy Spirit is because we give God the best part of our lives. I believe it comes when we give Him the run of the house, and we give Him the key, not to the best room but to the worst room; not only to the front room but to the basement. Give Him the whole bunch of keys and say, "Here they are, Lord. It is all open before Thee. If you find anything here contrary to Your will, I will put it out and will yield it." God will fill that home and fill that heart with an experience as real as any, and second only to salvation.' "

The measure in which the Holy Spirit lives within us depends entirely upon us. We can give Him only a part of our lives, or we can give Him all. Our lives are like houses. Some rooms are filled with activities, pleasures, friendships which may or may not be acceptable to God. Personal ambitions and unholy desires may occupy others.

God's Spirit is gracious, sensitive, courteous. He never enters a room where He is not welcome. You make the decision as to the number of rooms in your life into which He will be welcomed.

THREE SIMPLE PROPOSITIONS

Consider three simple propositions. Understanding and believing them can lead you to the blessed life that is hid with Christ in God.

First, the Holy Spirit indwells every child of God. Through the initial operation of the Spirit the mysterious change, the new birth, takes place. We are "born of the Spirit."

Second, the fullness of the Spirit is not experienced by every child of God. They have not received Him in fullness.

Third, the fullness of the Spirit may be experienced by every child of God. This is the baptism in the Holy Spirit.

A COMMAND

The Bible says, "Be filled with the Spirit" (Ephesians 5:18). This is not an option; it is a command. Thus the act of personal disobedience by the believer is involved.

This blessed doctrine is not to be taken lightly. God intends that His children shall be filled with His

Spirit. The Apostolic Church was a church of Spirit-baptized believers. The New Testament writers never thought in terms of a "non-Spirit-baptized" Christian. It never occurred to the apostles to divide believers into two groups—the filled and the unfilled. If, through lack of knowledge, believers had not entered into the fullness of the Spirit, immediate steps were taken to correct the situation (Acts 8:15; 9:17; 19:1-6). The order of the day was to get people converted and proceed immediately to lead them into the fullness of the Spirit.

BIBLICAL NAMES FOR THE EXPERIENCE

We can be quite clear about the scriptural terms used for the baptism of the Holy Spirit, for in the first two chapters of Acts the promised blessing is described in five equivalent phrases which are repeated elsewhere. These are:

(1) "The baptism in the Holy Ghost" (Acts 1:5; Luke 3:16; John 1:33; Acts 11:16).

(2) The Spirit "coming upon" or "falling upon" the believer (Acts 1:8; 2:17,18; 8:16; 10:44; 11:15).

(3) Individuals were "filled with the Holy Ghost" (Acts 2:4; 4:31; 9:17; Luke 3:22; 4:1,14,18).

(4) "Receiving the gift of the Holy Ghost" (Acts 2:38; 8:17-20; 10:45,47; 11:16,17).

(5) "The promise of the Father" (Acts 1:4; 2:33, 39; Luke 24:49).

LOTS OF QUESTIONS

The doctrine of the baptism in the Holy Spirit is receiving increased attention throughout the church world. Much confused theological thought on the doctrine has been existent throughout this century. Note some of the questions asked. Is the baptism in the Holy Spirit synonymous with conversion? Is it not sanctification? Is the experience an afterthought with God in His plan of the ages? Is it a part of the New

Testament Christianity? How important is the Baptism? Is it a spiritual luxury? How does one receive the baptism in the Holy Spirit? How may one know that he is baptized in the Holy Spirit?

The answers to these questions are found in the Scriptures. God's answer is needed, for personal opinion can be prejudiced and fallacious.

We can agree with many of the beliefs held by much of the church world about the person and work of the Holy Spirit. But our concern here is what is meant by the baptism in the Holy Spirit. Let us first approach the question from the negative side.

NOT CONVERSION

The baptism in the Holy Spirit is not regeneration. There is general agreement that the statement, "For by one Spirit are we all baptized into one body" (1 Corinthians 12:13), refers to the act of the Holy Spirit whereby He places the believer into the body of Christ. This is what happens as one is born of the Spirit (John 3:5-7).

While the Holy Spirit indwells all true believers (Romans 8:9), it does not follow that all believers are Spirit-filled. Believers are baptized into the body of Christ by the Holy Spirit; the Holy Spirit is the Agent. On the other hand, Christ is the Agent who baptizes us with the Holy Spirit (Matthew 3:11; John 1:33; Acts 2:33; Luke 24:49). This experience is called the "promise of (the) Father."

Peter's sermon at Pentecost evidences a concept of two separate events: (1) "Repent, and be baptized . . ." and (2) "ye shall receive the gift of the Holy Ghost" (Acts 2:38). The converts at Samaria had believed and were baptized and received the Holy Spirit later (Acts 8:12,17). The same is true of the converts at Ephesus (Acts 19:1-7).

NOT SANCTIFICATION

Sanctification is an operation of the Holy Spirit through the Word of God (John 15:3; 17:17). God counts us holy from the moment we are saved from sin and separated unto Him (1 Corinthians 1:2; 6:11; Acts 20:32; 26:18). Sanctification is: (1) positional and instantaneous, and (2) practical and progressive. Through appropriation by faith in the provision of Christ (Hebrews 10:10; Romans 6:6,11,13), through the power of the Spirit (Romans 8:1,2), and by the cleansing of the Word (John 15:3; 17:17), we become more like Christ. Sin is never defensible. We cannot expect God to keep us in holiness if we deliberately and knowingly place ourselves in circumstances which make it impossible.

PLANNED BY GOD

More than 400 years before the outpouring of the Spirit on the Day of Pentecost, the prophet Joel had spoken of the event (Joel 2:28,29; Acts 2:16). Some 700 years before that day Isaiah had prophesied concerning the outpouring (Isaiah 28:9-12; 1 Corinthians 14:21).

WHAT IS THE BAPTISM?

The baptism in the Holy Spirit is an *experience*. Baptism in water is an experience; so is the baptism in the Spirit. John the Baptist announced that Jesus would baptize His followers "with the Holy Ghost" (Matthew 3:11). Jesus reminded His disciples of John's prediction just before His ascension (Acts 1: 5). Peter never forgot this promise and referred to it when reporting to the brethren in Jerusalem of his experience in Cornelius' house. He said, "The Holy Ghost fell on them, as on us at the beginning. Then remembered I the word of the Lord." Peter went on to enlarge on the prediction of John and promise of

Jesus concluding, "What was I, that I could withstand God?" (Acts 11:15-17).

The baptism in the Spirit is a *gift*. It is not one of the Spirit's gifts; the Spirit himself is a gift from God. Jesus spoke of the Holy Spirit as a *gift* (Luke 11:13). Peter spoke of the *Gift* at Pentecost (Acts 2:38), in the house of Cornelius (Acts 10:45), and in testimony at Jerusalem (Acts 11:17).

The baptism in the Spirit is an *enduement* of power. Jesus promised that the Holy Spirit would clothe with power (Luke 24:49; Acts 1:8, RSV). The experience of the apostles abundantly illustrated this. Look at them before and after Pentecost.

THE PURPOSE OF THE BAPTISM

The baptism in the Holy Spirit is not a goal for the believer; it is a gateway to a fuller and richer spiritual life. It does not follow that one who is filled with the Spirit has reached the highest level of spirituality. The Baptism can be likened to the crossing of the Jordan by the Children of Israel. Before the Israelites was a land of milk and honey to be possessed and a land of enemies to be conquered. The infilling of the Spirit opens a promised land for the believer. It is not the culmination of Christian experience but the beginning of an exciting "life in the Spirit" (Galatians 5:25). The Holy Spirit comes to abide as a Companion, Helper, and Source of Strength (John 14:16-18).

The purpose of the baptism in the Spirit can be answered in a few words. "He shall glorify me," said Jesus (John 16:14). This is an all-inclusive expression. It includes the transformation of the individual (2 Corinthians 3:18), training to develop ability in the service of the Lord, and power to perform the task to which he is called.

Jesus said, "Ye shall receive power, after that the

Holy Ghost is come upon you: and ye shall be witnesses unto me" (Acts 1:8). Note, "ye shall receive" and "ye shall be." The purpose and the power of the Pentecostal experience can be summarized in the words *power to witness.* There is a distinction in the Greek between the two words rendered *power* in the English. One means "authority"; the other means "ability"—literally *dunamis.* The word *power* appears about 155 times in the King James Version of the New Testament. It is translated from the Greek word *dunamis* 69 times. The word has the meaning of "supernatural ability" and "strength." This is the meaning of *power to witness.* It is not merely the authority to witness, but the ability, the supernatural ability, to witness. There is divine equipment to witness; a divine energy—nothing less than God himself in the person of the Holy Spirit coming upon the believer to enable him to effectively witness of the Lord Jesus Christ.

IS THE BAPTISM FOR ALL BELIEVERS?

Some Christians apparently consider the baptism in the Spirit a luxury rather than a necessity. They view the experience as desirable but optional.

According to the Scriptures, the Baptism is for all believers (John 7:37-39). Jesus said, "If any man. . . ." It is obvious that He meant all men when He said, "He that believeth on me." All are included; no one is excluded.

Furthermore, the Scriptures indicate that Jesus commanded His disciples not to depart from Jerusalem until they had been filled with the Spirit (Acts 1:4,5). In like manner, Paul used imperative language when he said, "Be filled with the Spirit" (Ephesians 5:18).

On the Day of Pentecost "they were *all* filled with

the Holy Ghost" (Acts 2:4). Later, as Peter preached to the crowd which gathered to behold this phenomenon, he said, ". . . ye shall receive the gift of the Holy Ghost. For the promise is unto you, and to your children, and to all that are afar off, even as many as the Lord our God shall call" (Acts 2:38,39).

The Bible clearly indicates that no believer need be left out. Among the "all" on the Day of Pentecost were: Peter, the impulsive one who denied the Saviour (Matthew 26:70-75); Thomas, the doubter (John 20:24-28); and James and John, the "sons of thunder," who were ready to call down fire from heaven (Luke 9:53,54). Regardless of weaknesses and failures, the Spirit fell on those who obeyed the command to "tarry until."

IT'S FOR YOU

The infilling of the Holy Spirit is a personal experience. A correct theological position is important, but the baptism in the Holy Spirit is more than a doctrine. It is an experience and has been that to multitudes who have not been too clear regarding the doctrine. The 120 received an overwhelming experience in God; they were completely immersed—spirit, soul, and body—in the Holy Spirit.

The promise of the infilling is very personal; it is to *you*. It is interesting and assuring to note the use of the personal pronoun again and again. "*He* that believeth on me . . . , out of *his* belly shall flow rivers of living water . . ." (John 7:37-39). "The Father . . . shall give *you* another Comforter" (John 14:16). "He dwelleth with *you*, and shall be in *you*" (John 14:17). "It is expedient for *you* . . . I will send him [the Comforter] unto *you*" (John 16:7). "He will guide *you* . . . and show *you*" (John 16:13, 14). "I send the promise of my Father upon *you*: but tarry *ye* . . . until *ye* be endued with power from on high" (Luke 24:49). "For the promise is unto *you,* and to *your* children" (Acts 2:39).

IS THE BAPTISM NECESSARY?

For salvation? No, for "being justified by faith, we have peace with God through our Lord Jesus Christ" (Romans 5:1).

For life and service? Yes! The hour demands from the Church two essentials: powerful evangelism without and personal holiness within. The Pentecostal experience is the God-provided dynamic to fulfill both essentials, but it needs to be a continuous experience. When Spirit-baptized persons fail to live in the Spirit, discredit is brought upon the Spirit and His experience.

Unbaptized believers may point at the failings of those who have been baptized in the Spirit. Yet the failure of some does not justify disobedience to the Lord's command, "Be filled with the Spirit." Let's make our comparisons with God, His Word, and His standards.

ON RECEIVING THE BAPTISM

The work of baptizing believers is God's work. The Bible does not emphasize how we should receive, but how God will give. "He will give." "He will send." "He will pour out." "He will baptize."

God meets those who hunger and thirst after Him (Matthew 5:6; Luke 1:53). The seeker is to ask with intense desire, and continually praise and bless God (Luke 24:53; Psalm 100:4).

Say now in your heart, "I must have this gift of my Heavenly Father." It is not a luxury; it is essential. If you think that you do not need the Baptism, that you can manage quite well without this experience, you will not receive. You must ask to receive and seek to find (Luke 11:9,10). Jesus promised that the Heavenly Father will "give the Holy Spirit to them that ask him" (Luke 11:13).

Believe that God is no respecter of persons. Millions have been filled with the Spirit. You have as much right to the promise as any believer. If the Lord gave this gift to others, He'll give it to you.

Once a person is converted he should become a candidate for the Baptism. The believers in Samaria were new converts when they received (Acts 8). The same was true with the apostle Paul (Acts 9) as was the case in the house of Cornelius (Acts 10).

Faith is essential if we are to receive anything from God. Speaking of the blessing of Abraham coming on the Gentiles through Christ, Paul states that it came that "we might receive the promise of the Spirit through *faith* (Galatians 3:14). The Galatians were reminded that they received the Spirit "*by the hearing of faith* (Galatians 3:5). And Jesus promised the Holy Spirit to them that believe: "But this spake he of the Spirit, which they that *believe* on him should receive" (John 7:39).

Acts 2:4 In Jerusalem at Pentecost
. " 8:17 Samaria, 1 yr. later
3. " 10:46 Caesarea, 8 yrs later
4. " 19:6 Ephesus, 23 yrs. later
5. " 9:17 & 1 Cor. 14:18 Paul
         Joel 2:28-32

7

The Proof!

The Christiansons, missionary friends from Sweden, went to an isolated area of Africa to bring the gospel to a people who were totally unevangelized. They were the only white people within miles. After a period of time lonesomeness increased. Oh, to be back in Sweden, to see loved ones and friends, and to hear their mother tongue again.

God rewarded their efforts with converts. The time came for the first water baptismal service. Coincidentally, the first convert was the first to be baptized. As he was being raised from the watery grave, he became the first to receive the baptism in the Holy Spirit.

Imagine the great joy which came to the lonely missionary couple as they heard the African national worshiping God in the Swedish language. Translated, his words were the equivalent of "Hail Him! Hail Him! Crown Him King of kings and Lord of lords." He continued at great length in expressions of praise and adulation in fluent Swedish.

DIVIDED OPINION

Most Christians recognize that the Scriptures teach an experience known as the baptism in the Holy Spirit. But opinion from there on is divided. First, when does the experience occur? Is it synonymous with or subsequent to conversion? That question was answered in the previous chapter.

Second, what constitutes the evidence so that a person can know he has received the experience?

We believe that the initial physical evidence of the baptism in the Spirit is speaking with other tongues, and we base our belief upon the Word of God.

Speaking in tongues was prophesied in both the Old and New Testaments. Isaiah foretold it, "For with stammering lips and another tongue will he speak to this people. To whom he said, This is the rest . . . and this is the refreshing . . ." (Isaiah 28: 11,12). That Isaiah made reference to the supernatural experience of speaking in tongues is beyond contradiction for Paul in his treatment of the subject refers to the Isaiah passage (1 Corinthians 14: 21).

In the New Testament Jesus himself foretold "they shall speak with new tongues" (Mark 16:17).

FIVE INSTANCES

In the Book of Acts there are five instances of the outpouring of the Spirit. Three are described in detail, one in part, and the other only inferred. These are our sole data to determine what happened when Christians were baptized in the Spirit in apostolic days.

WHERE IT ALL BEGAN

The first account is that of the Day of Pentecost. The 120 were gathered in obedience to await the "promise of the Father." Without preconceived notions and prejudices, they surely had no idea what would happen. Yet, when suddenly the Holy Spirit fell upon them "they were all filled with the Holy

Ghost, and began to speak with other tongues, as the Spirit gave them utterance" (Acts 2:4). This is the fullest account. The experience was signalized by the external signs of wind and fire and the internal sign of speaking with other tongues. All were filled and all spoke in tongues. There were no exceptions. In this instance the speakers spoke in tongues unknown to themselves, but known to their hearers.

SPECTACULAR HAPPENING

The next account is of the outpouring in Samaria (Acts 8:14-17). There is no mention of tongues, but there was spectacular evidence. Something convinced Simon, the astute sorcerer, that the converts at Samaria had received the Holy Spirit. The terminology used is similar—"receive" and "fallen upon." The methods are similar—the laying on of hands. Adam Clarke and Matthew Henry, to cite two of many, state that the Samaritans received the Holy Spirit and spoke with tongues.

WHAT ABOUT PAUL?

Instance number three is recorded in Acts 9 and has to do with Paul's experience. The Bible does not say that he spoke with tongues there, nor does it say that he didn't. But of one thing we are sure, and that is that he did speak with tongues. He states, "I thank my God, I speak with tongues more than ye all" (1 Corinthians 14:18). Even though only the deliverance from his blindness is specifically mentioned, the commission of Ananias to Paul (Acts 9: 17) would not have been completely fulfilled had he not been "filled with the Holy Ghost."

INTERRUPTING THE SERMON

The fourth Biblical record is of the outpouring

on the Gentiles (Acts 10:44-46). While Peter was preaching "the Holy Ghost fell on all them which heard the word." How did Peter know? "For they heard them speak with tongues, and magnify God."

TWENTY-THREE YEARS LATER

The final account records the experience at Ephesus (Acts 19). Although this is 23 years after the first outpouring of the Spirit at Pentecost, again there was the evidence accompanying the reception of the Spirit. "And when Paul had laid his hands upon them, the Holy Ghost came on them; and they spake with tongues, and prophesied" (v. 6).

WIND ... FIRE ... TONGUES ...

A review of these cases shows us that a highly mystical and charismatic experience is involved. Certain phenomena accompanied the infilling of the Spirit. They were: wind (Acts 2:2); fire (Acts 2:3); speaking in tongues (Acts 2:4; 10:46; 19:6); magnification of God (Acts 10:46); and prophecy (Acts 19:6).

The phenomena describing the advent of the Holy Spirit in the first three verses of the second chapter of Acts (wind and fire) are nowhere repeated or referred to in the rest of the New Testament. These two demonstrations had occurred before Pentecost, whereas speaking with tongues was distinctly a Pentecost and post-Pentecost experience. The "rushing mighty wind" and the "cloven tongues like as of fire" were external to the disciples and in the realm of nature; speaking with tongues was a personal experience in which the recipients were involved. The wind and the fire preceded the filling of the 120; speaking with tongues came as a result of the filling. The wind and fire were natural forces, not of human volition. Speaking with tongues involved the yielding of human will. Human will is an obstacle of God's own creation, one that He never violates. God always requires human volition to accomplish His purposes in us. We will never be filled with the Spirit, never speak with tongues, until we yield our whole being—mental, physical, vocal, and spiritual faculties —to God.

The other phenomena (other than tongues), that appeared at outpourings of the Spirit were prophesying and magnification of God. Each is mentioned only once—prophesying at Ephesus and magnifying God at Cornelius' house.

AUTHENTICATING EVIDENCE

In the Book of Acts speaking with tongues is the authenticating evidence of the baptism in the Holy Spirit, just as prophecy, wisdom, discernment, healing, miracles, and casting out of demons were under the old covenant; but never before had anyone spoken in tongues (at Babel the new tongues became the native languages of the speakers).

In three of the five cases in Acts it is distinctly stated that the recipients of the Baptism spoke with tongues, while in the fourth the implication is so strong as to leave no reasonable doubt that they did so. And there is no question but what the recipient in the fifth case, the apostle Paul, was a speaker in tongues on the basis of his own testimony.

The Scriptures require the testimony of "two . . . or three witnesses" (Deuteronomy 17:6) to establish a fact. Lest there be any doubt, the Book of Acts provides five witnesses (accounts) that those who were baptized spoke with other tongues.

START WITH THE BEGINNING

Beginnings are important. The Bible refers very

specifically to some beginnings. To illustrate, Peter referred to the beginning when reporting on the happenings in the household of Cornelius, ". . . the Holy Ghost fell on them, as on us at the beginning" (Acts 11:15).

The beginning of the Pentecostal phenomenon occurred on the Day of Pentecost. For this reason we go back to this beginning. In this instance a precedent was established. A precedent is a first occurrence which becomes a pattern to guide the future. Precedence has only to do with that which may be repeated. The 120 received an experience which, according to our Lord and His Word, is available to all of His followers. Therefore, we look back to the Day of Pentecost for precedence, for a pattern of evidence. The evidence that the Holy Spirit had filled the believers at Pentecost was their speaking with tongues. Thus, we believe that speaking in tongues is evidence of the same experience today. The cumulative testimony of the instances recorded in the Book of Acts where the gift of the Spirit was received bears out the fact of the continuing evidence as at the beginning.

Other matters of precedence established at Pentecost include:

1. The baptism in the Holy Spirit was to be for the entire Church, not only for leaders.

2. Spiritual experiences may not always be understood by those outside the Church.

3. Anointed preaching was to be the major means of evangelism.

4. The power of the Holy Spirit was to enable the Church to reach large numbers of people.

A PATTERN PROVIDED

The happenings on the Day of Pentecost set the pattern for us. Acts 2:4 is set as the unique pattern for the baptism in the Spirit, and is the master key that fits all the subsequent manifestations of the Spirit in the Book of Acts and in the Epistles.

Moses was admonished of God when building the tabernacle, "See . . . that thou make all things according to the pattern showed to thee in the mount" (Hebrews 8:5). After he had carefully done this the glory of God filled the completed structure. In like manner, our physical bodies become the temple of the Holy Spirit (1 Corinthians 3:16; 6:19). When we follow the pattern, God's power and glory will fill us.

Note these things about the pattern:

1. They were *all* filled with the Spirit—it was for all.

2. They were all *filled*—this same term is expressed in a variety of synonymous terms, each of them indicating fullness.

3. They were all filled with *the* Holy Ghost. In the Greek the article *the* is omitted. This is not an insignificant omission or error, but it is the inspired Word of God. The name of the Holy Spirit requires the article when He is spoken of in himself; but, when the reference is to His manifestations in men, the article is omitted. For example, in Acts 1:5 Jesus said, "Ye shall be baptized with the Holy Ghost," and the article is not in the Greek. On the other hand it appears in John 14:26 ". . . the Holy Ghost . . . shall teach you all things."

Here lies an important truth. We are filled with the Spirit, but we receive only a measure of the Spirit, the Giver being greater than the gift. Jesus was the only One who received the Spirit without measure. "Of his fullness have all we received, and grace for grace" (John 1:16). Thus we need one measure of grace to replenish another. Constant fresh infillings are needed. Keep on being filled.

4. "They were all filled . . . and began to speak with

69

other tongues." This was spontaneous. It was vocal. It was the initial evidence. The word translated *to speak* simply means "to talk." It never means "to preach." The hearers were "amazed" and "wondered." Some were "in doubt" while others "mocked." It was Peter's anointed preaching in the power of the Spirit that won the 3,000 converts.

5. They were filled . . . other tongues, as the *Spirit gave them utterance. Utterance* as translated from the Greek means "to speak plainly," "to declare." It's the same verb used by Peter in Acts 2:14 when he "lifted up his voice, and *said*. . . ." Paul uses it in Acts 26:25 when he replies to Festus, "I am not mad . . . but *speak forth* the words of truth and soberness."

Vincent says that utterance is "a peculiar word, and purposely chosen to denote the clear, loud utterance under the miraculous impulse." Trench says it means "the articulate utterance of human language." The utterance was of articulate, if not intelligible speech.

SAME BUT DIFFERENT

The speaking in tongues at the time of being filled with the Spirit is the same in essence as the gift of tongues (1 Corinthians 12:4,10,28), but different in purpose and use.

We speak of tongues as the initial, physical evidence. Quickly we recognize that the words *initial* and *physical* are not taken from the Scriptures. We use them just for what they are, for purposes of definition. Speaking in tongues is the initial evidence of the Baptism, and it is a physical evidence.

WHY TONGUES?

Why did God choose tongues as the evidence? Speech is the distinctively characteristic manifestation of human personality. In the whole creative order, it is a uniquely human faculty. Thurneysen underscores it with perception, "The mystery of speech is identical with the mystery of personality, with the image of God in man."

But what's so good about other tongues? Unnecessary . . . ridiculous . . . irrational . . . far out? No, it's Biblical. But why not our own languages? The answer is found in the asking. When I speak English, I'm speaking words that are in my own mind, words that manifest my personality. When I speak in tongues as the Holy Spirit gives utterance, I speak words that are in the mind of the Spirit, words that manifest His personality, words uncensored by my mind, words that are a beautiful self-manifestation of the Spirit.

The two last faculties to be surrendered are man's mind and his tongue. In speaking in an unknown tongue, the mind and the tongue are completely given over to the Spirit. As in water baptism the candidate yields to the baptizer until completely immersed in water, so in the Spirit's baptism the seeker yields to Christ until completely given over to the Spirit.

While there are other evidences of the baptism in the Holy Spirit besides speaking in an unknown tongue, we must admit that this one sign was chosen in divine wisdom. No other evidence so sufficiently and conclusively satisfies the recipient and the witnesses present, as does this as an initial evidence.

I reemphasize the truth that the baptism in the Spirit was the normal experience in the Apostolic Church. All believers are entitled to and should ardently expect and earnestly seek for the "promise of the Father." It is important that all who receive be able to describe the experience, and pointing back to the Day of Pentecost say, "This is that!"

8

You Can Receive

How can I receive the baptism in the Holy Spirit? That's a good question and an honest one asked by many very sincere people. The answer is simple yet profound. There's only one way to receive the Holy Spirit, and that's in the New Testament way!

When you are filled with the Spirit, in the New Testament way, you'll know it. You won't need anyone else to tell you. You can say what the little boy said to the traveling salesman who had questioned the lad as to the distance and direction to the next town, plus several other questions. The boy was backward and bashful, and his answer to each question was, "I don't know." Finally the salesman in disgust said, "Well, don't you know anything?" "Yes," said the boy, "I know where I'm going and I know I'm not lost."

A RIGHT WAY

There's a right way and a wrong way to seek for spiritual power. It's not that God is unwilling to give the Holy Spirit. Far from it. We know that God is more ready to give than we are to receive. Delay in an answer to your petition is not God's fault; there must be another reason.

I read of a boy with a questioning mind who wondered for a long time what caused the wind to blow.

After pondering the matter at length, he arrived at what he thought was the logical reason. He concluded that the movements of the branches caused the air current, for when the branches were moving the wind was blowing. Not until he was older did he discover his folly.

It seems that a lot of folk use that kind of reasoning regarding the baptism in the Spirit. Some think that you receive the Spirit by shaking; others believe you must kneel. Still others believe you can't receive unless you lie prostrate. Because the infilling is accompanied by speaking in an unknown tongue, don't think tongues brings the Holy Spirit.

GET WITH IT

There's no virtue in long waiting. You don't need to tarry for years. Make a virtue of earning the Baptism by doing, and you're not receiving a gift.

A lady had been seeking the fullness of the Spirit for a long time. A minister attempted to help her. She curtly responded, "Don't you try to tell me how to do this. I've been at it for years."

There are simple conditions to follow, for the baptism in the Spirit is not the culmination of a lengthy and difficult time of spiritual conflict. The Baptism is not the prize for an almost unending period of penance and soul travail. The experience is not a goal. It's not an end, but a beginning; it's not an achievement attained as an award, but a gateway to a life in the Spirit.

For two reasons it's impossible for us to reach that certain level of holiness where we merit the Holy Spirit. First, the Bible is unequivocal concerning the fact that the shed blood of Christ is our only means of approach to God. Second, the Baptism is a gift.

The prominence of the word *gift* in the Bible is

not incidental—not a play on words. It's tremendously important that we understand that the baptism in the Spirit is a gift.

If a friend presents a gift to me it would be an insult to him for me to insist on paying for it. I'd violate his act of love. A gift is something given to me, not a reward for my effort. If I must earn it, it's not a gift.

A COMMAND ... A PROMISE ... A GIFT

To be filled with the Holy Spirit means a command is to be obeyed, a promise is to be claimed, and a gift is to be received. The experience is a gift to be received, not a reward to achieve.

While the Bible has much to say about the baptism in the Spirit, it has little to say about how we may receive the experience. We gain most of our instruction by observing what the disciples were told to do.

TARRY

The disciples were told to "tarry," which literally means to "sit down" and to remain there for a purpose. They "all continued with one accord in prayer and supplication" (Acts 1:14).

REPENT

Peter exhorted his listeners to "Repent . . . and ye shall receive the gift of the Holy Ghost" (Acts 2:38). Conviction of *sin* brings us to the Saviour. It's awful to see sin still having dominion over you—ugly weeds that choke the harvest, lack of a meek and quiet spirit, pride, self-centeredness, envy, roots of bitterness. You resolve. You strive. You pray. You do penance. The frustration seems devastating.

Your losses seem beyond recouping—evil thoughts harbored, questionable actions taken, wrong words spoken, duties neglected, usefulness impaired, joy lacking. Peter remembered his cowardice, his lies, his denial of the One who meant all to him. Thomas remembered his doubtings. James and John, the "sons of thunder," remembered their tempers.

THIRST

Conviction of *want* makes us thirst and pant after God. The Lord meets those who hunger and thirst after Him (Matthew 5:6; Luke 1:53). Jesus declared that we must thirst for the inner floods of the Spirit (John 7:37-39). Are you thirsty for more of God, so much so that indeed the rivers of His divine fullness only will satisfy? When you are really thirsty, greatly desiring this rich bounty of God-given abundance, you are well on the way to receiving. The Psalmist said, "As the hart panteth after the water brooks, so panteth my soul after thee, O God" (Psalm 42:1). That's an expression of the soul yearning for satisfaction.

FOCUS ON GOD

Thirst and hunger after God! Don't be ashamed of it! Don't deny soul thirst and hunger. Let it possess you, dominate you!

Some people get very discouraged because they do not receive the fullness of the Spirit. The reason they do not receive is that they are self-centered. Fix your eyes on Jesus. Set your affections and thoughts on Him. Crave after God.

OBEY

God gives the Holy Spirit "to them that obey him" (Acts 5:32). As C. M. Ward states, "Obedience is not picking and choosing." When Jesus told the disciples to "tarry . . . in . . . Jerusalem, until" (Luke 24:49), it was their job to do so. And that's exactly what they did. They could have debated it. Why not get alone in a quiet country place out in the midst of the beauties of God's creation, or down by Galilee in the old familiar places. Or, it's hard to get away from home and family responsibilities; why can't I tarry at home? What a host of arguments we raise.

But they didn't debate; they didn't argue. They obeyed! Insubordination and rebellion will always withhold God's blessing. We can't dictate to God. Disobedience will rob us. Jesus said, "Jerusalem" and Jerusalem it was. As they obeyed, they were not disappointed. We say they obeyed, but only 120 did so. Five hundred received the command to tarry in Jerusalem for the promise of the Father. Only 120 obeyed, and only 120 received.

George accepted Christ as Saviour on a Sunday afternoon. He eagerly responded to encouragement to seek for the baptism in the Holy Spirit. Something strange thing happened. A figure of $.80 began to appear before him. Every time he came to pray, there was the $.80. It was a reminder of an incident in boyhood days.

In his early teens George had delivered a load of pigs to the local hog buyer. He was aware of the price his father agreed upon—an even amount of $50. The buyer gave him a draw slip on his bank; but the amount looked like $50.80. The bank gave George $50.80. Temptation overcame him. He gave the $50 to his father and kept the $.80.

The incident had long since been forgotten. He prided himself on his honesty. Now the Holy Spirit was reminding him of a flaw. He found no peace until he sent a letter with the $.80 back to his home community in another state. And shortly he was filled with the Holy Spirit. "To obey is better than sacrifice" (1 Samuel 15:22).

Faith is the chief qualification for anyone to be filled with the Spirit; we must believe. "That we might receive the promise of the Spirit *through faith*" (Galatians 3:14). "The [Holy] Spirit, which they that *believe* on him should receive" (John 7:39). "He that cometh to God must *believe* that he is, and that he is a rewarder of them that diligently seek him" (Hebrews 11:6). Jesus said, "What things soever ye desire, when ye pray, *believe* that ye receive them, and ye shall have them" (Mark 11:24).

Faith is the condition on which God bestows all His gifts—salvation, sanctification, healing, the gifts of the Spirit. Faith is the hand that reaches out to God and never returns empty.

Begging and pleading is not faith. "Faith cometh by hearing, and hearing by the word of God" (Romans 10:17). Faith is more than just accepting God's Word as true; it is an act. James declares, "Let him ask in faith, nothing wavering: for he that wavereth is like a wave of the sea driven with the wind and tossed. For let not that man think that he shall receive any thing of the Lord" (James 1:6,7).

Faith is more than waiting on God; faith accepts. Hebrews 11:1 contains what is generally used as a definition of faith. Weymouth's rendering is, "Now faith is a confident *assurance* of that for which we hope, a *conviction* of the reality of things which we do not see." Goodspeed's translation is, "Faith means the *assurance* of what we hope for; it is our *conviction* about things that we cannot see." The words *conviction* and *assurance* are also used in the Revised Standard Version: "Now faith is the *assurance* of things hoped for, the *conviction* of things not seen." The Amplified uses the words "*assurance* (the confirmation, the title-deed) . . . *conviction* of their reality— faith perceiving as real fact what is not revealed to the senses." The Living Bible paraphrases with ". . . confident *assurance* that something we want is going to happen. It is the certainty that what we hope for is waiting for us . . ."

Faith is expectation. Anticipation is lively. Praising the Lord helps us to be in a receiving attitude. Praise strengthens faith. Many are filled while their hands are lifted in adoration and praise.

TAKE

Finally, the seeker after the things of God is urged to "take." Revelation 22:17 states, "And whosoever will, let him take of the water of life freely." This word *take* is the word that is translated *receive* in the passages relating to receiving the Spirit.

Paul used the word when he stated, "We also joy in God through our Lord Jesus Christ, by whom we have now *received* the atonement" (Romans 5:11).

Peter used the word when he declared, "Repent, and be baptized . . . and ye shall *receive* the gift of the Holy Ghost" (Acts 2:38).

John used the word when he said, "As many as *received* him, to them gave he power to become the sons of God" (John 1:12).

The question of posture arises. As stated earlier, the disciples were told to "tarry," which literally means to "sit down" and to remain there for a purpose. On the Day of Pentecost they were sitting. Biblical instances of posture in prayer are varied: standing (1 Kings 8:22; Mark 11:25); bowing down (Psalm 95:6); kneeling (2 Chronicles 6:13; Psalm 95:6; Luke 22:41; Acts 20:36); falling on the face (Numbers 16:22; Joshua 5:14; 1 Chronicles 21:16; Mathew 26:39); spreading forth the hands (Isaiah 1:15; 2 Chronicles 6:13); lifting up the hands (Psalm 28:2; Lamentations 2:19; 1 Timothy 2:8).

The 120 at Pentecost were sitting. The Samaritans received after Peter and John laid their hands on them. Cornelius and his house received while listening to Peter preach. The Ephesians received after Paul had instructed them, baptized them, and laid his hands on them.

The attitude of the heart is more important than the posture of the body. The Bible does not indicate a set pattern; circumstances are of little consequence.

COME HOLY SPIRIT

While I was preaching in Recife, Brazil several were filled with the Spirit during the sermon—an experience such as Peter had, and one that I had secretly prayed for over a period of years.

I know homemakers who have received while at the kitchen sink. Several to my knowledge were filled while in bed during the night.

Jess Locket was worshiping God while plowing. He reached for the hand clutch to stop the tractor. As he did so he was prostrated in the field between the tractor and the plow and began to speak with other tongues as the Spirit gave him utterance.

Mildred Wold came to our meetings as a Christian from another church background. She had been warned against the Pentecostal experience. She enjoyed the spirit of the services and finally prayed, "Lord, if this experience is of You, show yourself to me." Kneeling at the altar, she had a vision of Christ. Her heart was overwhelmed, and shortly she began to speak in an unknown tongue.

Some people receive while standing, kneeling, or sitting; some are alone, while others are in a crowded prayer meeting. I received the baptism of the Holy Spirit lying flat on my back. The Lord's dealing with you may be entirely different.

WHO DOES THE SPEAKING?

Another question is often raised: With whom **does** speaking in tongues originate—the Christian or the Holy Spirit? Speaking in tongues orginates with the Holy Spirit. But God does not force His gifts upon you. You must yield to the Spirit and speak out as you feel the Spirit prompting you.

You furnish the voice; the Spirit supplies the utterance. If the Spirit spoke through you, and you had no control, the Spirit would be forcing himself upon you instead of leading you. You would no longer be a free moral agent but would be coerced to do that over which you had no control.

MY EXPERIENCE

From my own experience I gained an understanding of what many earnest people go through. I desperately desired the fullness of the Spirit. Somehow I had the idea that when the Spirit took over my own response would be inactive. Again and again I would sense the mighty power of God upon me, but I would throttle His manifestation for fear that self was involved. One day I let go—waves of power, peace, joy, and blessing engulfed me. I seemed to be lifted out of this world, out of self into the very presence of our Heavenly Father and the Lord Jesus Christ, our blessed Saviour. I spoke in unknown tongues at great length. I trembled like a leaf in the wind. Every member of my being was submerged in God.

That was my experience. Yours may be different, and very likely will be.

The promise is for you! Don't settle for less!

9
Don't Lose Your Key

You get a call from your automobile dealer. He's got great news—your new car is ready at last. You check the equipment you ordered—it's all there. The color's right. Yes, the upholstery is just what you want. You look under the hood—she's a beaut. Kick the tires—you've always got to do that when looking at a new car—apparently it does something; if you know, please tell me. You open the doors—yep, they shut tightly. The turn signals are okay. The radio—say, that quadraphonic sound is something. All's perfect!

The dealer says, "Take 'er away." You slip behind the wheel. It's just a great feeling—everything smells new. But something's wrong. "The key, the key, what did I do with the key?" you ask yourself. Somehow in your excitement you've mislaid the key.

Gas in the tank, good rubber, new motor, beautiful body, power available—but it's all to no avail, all wasted without the key. You can't even drive it off the lot.

In the experience of the baptism in the Holy Spirit, God gave you the key. The fullness of the Spirit is the key that connects your Christian life with the source of heaven's power.

LOST YOUR KEY?

You've been filled with the Holy Spirit. What a

beautiful experience. Like your new car, it's just what you wanted. But then something happens; your spiritual life and power seem to drain away. You've lost some of the victory and power; you've lost your key.

Some people lose their keys; others never use the key. I saw a car 25 years old with about 1,000 miles on the odometer. The owner bought it for transportation but never did use it. He planned to save it for the day he really needed a good car. It was an investment that never was beneficial in daily life.

ON EATING APPLES

Michael Horban tells of the little old lady whose one tree produced a crop of excellent apples. The apples looked so perfect that she decided they were too good to eat. So, she wrapped them individually and packed them in a barrel. Day after day she'd go to the storage room to admire her wonderful apples. She wouldn't eat them—just look at them.

One day the little old lady saw a brown spot on one of the apples—it was spoiling; so, she ate it. Then another apple had a spot—she ate that one. One by one the apples spoiled. The little old lady ate the entire barrel—one spoiled apple after another. She never did enjoy a single good apple. Not too smart, you say. But we're like that in many ways.

In the baptism in the Holy Spirit, God has given us a great source of power for victorious living and effective witnessing. What we do after receiving is extremely important.

NO NEED FOR AN ENERGY CRISIS

Paul writes to the Philippians about "the supply of the Spirit" (1:19). In the Comforter or Enabler we not only have an abundant, but a superabundant supply of energy. That's the plus of the Spirit.

One of the great weaknesses is that we center too

much on ourselves, and far too little on the Holy Spirit. For this reason many Christians have a shallow, frustrated walk. They may be earnest, but totally lacking in radiant living.

A DOORWAY

The baptism in the Holy Spirit is not the climax of the Spirit-filled life, but rather the doorway to a walk by the Spirit which ever increases in blessing and service. When you receive the fullness of the Spirit you are not to relax and feel now you've attained, this is it. You have merely crossed Jordan; before you lies Canaan, the promised land. Canaan was the land of milk and honey, grapes of Eshcol and corn, but it also was the land with enemies, including great giants and walled cities, all needing to be conquered.

Bear in mind, the Baptism does not make you perfect. Possibly, when urging believers to seek the infilling of the Spirit, claims have been made which raise the expectations concerning the Spirit-filled life and go beyond the claims of the Scriptures.

NO SUPERMEN

We are prone to believe that the men of the Bible who were so greatly used of God were special creations, when in reality they lived rather normal lives. Despite their knowledge and experience of the supernatural manifestations of the Holy Spirit, they experienced the norms of hunger and thirst, weariness and pain, cold and nakedness. Paul's testimony is a good example (2 Corinthians 11:23-27). On the whole, they were men "subject to like passions as we are" (James 5:17).

Yet, despite the normality of their lives and experiences, men such as Peter and Paul, James and John lived by standards for the Christian life which were far beyond anything which the natural man could attain. The continuing indwelling presence of the Holy Spirit was the secret.

MEETING IT HEAD-ON

The obstacles which you confront as a Christian in your daily walk are massive and frontal. You live in a world system which is utterly contrary to the things of God. Constant pressure is on you to compromise with the world and conform to it.

In addition to the world itself, you encounter Satan as your archenemy. This battle is for real. You are not wrestling with flesh and blood (Ephesians 6:11-18) but with satanic powers. Satan not only blinds the minds of unbelievers (2 Corinthians 4:4), but he comes as a roaring lion to scare the wits out of you and to devour you (1 Peter 5:8). Jesus said the devil is a liar and a murderer (John 8:44) and is exceedingly deceptive, often appearing as an angel of light (2 Corinthians 11:14). Human wisdom and power can't match him. There's only one way to defeat him —through appropriating the victory of Christ over him by the power of the Spirit.

You face another problem in addition to the world and Satan. You struggle with your own inner weakness. Although you have a new nature and a new life in Christ, the old nature is still there. From time to time it tries to assert itself and gain control. This is the struggle Paul writes about in Romans 6 and 7.

IS THERE NO HOPE?

Both experiences and Scripture demonstrate that we are beset by constant temptation and opposition to the holy life. We could never even partially attain God's high standard of conduct apart from the grace and power of the Holy Spirit.

Having said all of this, I want to state further that the spiritual life is not a great and continual struggle.

There is conflict! Our position of victory, however, is found by living in Romans 8 and not chapter 7.

God does not intend for you to live under a cloud of condemnation. The Spirit comes to free you from fear and bondage.

A lot of people are like the poor Japanese soldier who struggled keeping body and soul together living in hiding for 30 years after World War II was over. He lived away from loved ones, friends, and homeland under the most abject, depressing conditions, unaware that peace had been declared three decades before.

There are others who attach a sort of impractical mysticism to spiritual life. They tend to compartmentalize the things of the Spirit, separating them from everyday life with its ups and downs, problems, and tasks. The Spirit is with us in the dark valleys as much as on the sunlit mountain heights.

The dominant theme of the great eighth chapter of Romans is the triumphant message of deliverance from sin by the power of the Holy Spirit. One of the great works of the Spirit is to bring us into a life of victory in Christ. Deliverance comes through the "law of the Spirit of life in Christ Jesus" (v. 2). As long as we remain in Him, we need fear no punishment, no doom, no purgatory. We are victorious in Christ to the extent that we "walk not after the flesh, but after the Spirit" (v. 4).

THE CONTACT PRINCIPLE

Motor vehicles run on the storage principle. The fuel tank becomes empty and must be refilled. The old streetcars ran on the contact principle; as long as contact was maintained with the wire, they moved. I remember riding one when the car stopped. The operator had to get out and get connected to the power line. Victory in your life depends upon maintaining contact with the Source of power.

That's called walking by the power of the Spirit. In contrast to the exhortations to "quench not the Spirit" or to "grieve not the Spirit," walking by the Spirit is a positive moment-by-moment dependence upon the Spirit and what He can empower you to do.

WALK, NOT HOP

Donald Gee makes a good point by saying, "The Lord never said, 'Hop in the Spirit' nor 'Skip in the Spirit,' but He did say 'Walk in the Spirit.' "

A life of walking in the Spirit is based on the Word of God. You can never grow spiritually apart from the Word. Strength comes through the Word; the Word provides you with spiritual vitamins. Let the Word be your manna in the morning (Job 23:12).

Furnish your mind with understanding (Ephesians 5:17). Feed your emotional life on a spiritual menu (Ephesians 5:18). Fill your volitional life with constructive, purposeful work and service (Ephesians 5:16).

THREE WAYS

Three means of keeping filled are listed in Ephesians 5:19-21. First, talk at length with each other about the Lord, using psalms, hymns, and spiritual songs, making music in your hearts to the Lord. Life in the Spirit is Christ-centered.

A heart of thanksgiving and praise is a second means of maintaining the fullness of the Spirit. "Giving thanks always for all things." Easy? Not always. Impractical? No. The spiritual person seeks to make all experiences—pleasant or unpleasant—steps on the ladder of spiritual growth.

The third means of keeping filled is "submitting yourselves one to another in the fear of God." This requires grace. Our flesh wants to feel worthy, desiring to be pampered and praised. The person who lives in the Spirit learns submission, first to God and then to others.

The Spirit works in us to produce fruit. Jesus said, "Ye have not chosen me, but I have chosen you, and ordained you, that ye should go and bring forth fruit, and that your fruit should remain" (John 15:16). The gifts of God are bestowed suddenly. We are saved the moment we believe. The Holy Spirit came to the 120 "suddenly." Even the gifts of the Spirit may be manifested in one's life through an immediate response. But the fruit of the Spirit comes only as we walk in the Spirit.

HOW'S YOUR ORCHARD?

The list of the fruit of the Spirit in Galatians 5:22, 23 depicts in vivid terms the Christ-life, life by the Spirit. All of this is latent in the incorruptible seed implanted in us at the new birth, but is made potent by the nurture and influence of the Holy Spirit as we yield our lives to Him.

Worthwhile noting is the fact that the Galatians list of fruit is nine in number, as is the list of spiritual gifts in 1 Corinthians 12:8-10. This suggests balance for our lives. Gifts and graces should have equal emphasis, the one being a manifestation of power, the other of life. The life that experiences the power of God with an accompanying enriching growth in grace is scripturally balanced. The divine ethic is made effective by the divine dynamic.

The first three fruits—love, joy, and peace—have to do with condition in relation to the individual.

The next three—long-suffering, gentleness, and goodness—deal with conduct in relation to our fellowmen.

The last three—faith, meekness, and temperance—speak of character and relation to God.

I have used the word *fruits* in the above statements. In reality the Scripture uses the singular fruit, but with various facets of manifestation. Paul does not use bad grammar when he says the fruit of the Spirit is love, joy, peace. The whole fruit is love, but love manifests itself in the variety of ways as listed.

WHAT A CONTRAST

The beauty of the fruit is enhanced when seen in contrast to the monstrous brood of the works of the flesh (Galatians 5:19-21). The works of the flesh total 17 in this listing by Paul. The words *"and such like"* indicate that he could have added scores more. Each one of the works of the flesh contends against another for an evil mastery. While the ninefold fruit of the Spirit issues from one life within, the works of the flesh are separate acts performed by man. The fruit is not many separate graces.

The Spirit can't produce His fruit apart from your cooperation. You are responsible for the walk in the Spirit; the Spirit is responsible for the fruit.

It has been said, "The problem of living a holy life in sinful flesh is a problem worthy of God." But as Gordon F. Atter has stated, "The fruit of the Spirit conquered where the thunders of Sinai had failed."

A LESSON FROM BIOLOGY

In biology we learn that life depends upon an adequate environment and a proper relation to that environment. Take any living thing out of its environment and it dies. The fish must have water. The polar bear must have ice if he's to be kept in the tropics. The seed must have soil, sun, and rain to produce life. An adequate environment is essential;

the more perfect the environment, the better are the chances for an organism to survive.

Not only does an organism need an adequate environment, it must relate to its environment. A vital connection with the surroundings is necessary. Uproot a plant and its withers and dies. The more completely the organism relates to its environment, the better are its chances to be productive. Place a tree with a poor root system in the wrong soil, add to it the problem of insufficient moisture, and it's doomed to die.

The First Epistle of John clearly shows us that the source of Christian living is in living in the love of God. The Holy Spirit is given to enable us to tap in on God's laws of life.

Our job is to maintain a relationship with the perfect environment of God's love. To this end the Holy Spirit helps us, for "the love of God is shed abroad in our hearts by the Holy Ghost which is given unto us" (Romans 5:5).

The Spirit-filled and thrilled life, rich in the fruit of the Spirit and overflowing with the full measure of God's love, will be the channel God can use. Zechariah put it succinctly, "Not by might, nor by power, but by my Spirit, saith the Lord of hosts" (4:6).

Acts 2:39

10
Concerning Spiritual Gifts
PART 1

At Pentecost the disciples received Pentecostal power to face the Pentecostal task. The Holy Spirit came after the believers stopped gazing upward at the skies of Mt. Olivet and made their way back to Jerusalem in obedience to their Master's command. They faced a world of need, danger, and opportunity.

God gave to the disciples—and to us—His power for an overwhelming task. He gives His power only to those who need it. We surely qualify for the "need" category; our weakness is God's opportunity. It's not a matter of psyching ourselves up or mimicking the experience of others. The disciples were not faking it at Pentecost; we need that same power, and it's available today.

Following Pentecost, the Holy Spirit began to bestow gifts upon individuals for the benefit of the Church and the extension of God's kingdom on earth. These gifts were not and never are given to be exploited for one's own ends, nor are they given for mere personal enjoyment.

The gifts of the Holy Spirit come from God. Coming from Him they are good. To criticize them is to criticize God. They are given in love; and, while the Lover is more important than His gifts, you can't separate Him from them. That would be like separating the gift of the wedding ring from the love of the bridegroom for his bride. For the bride to criticize the ring, to decline to accept it at the wedding, or to refuse to wear it after the ceremony is inconceivable.

LOOK INSIDE THE WRAPPINGS

An English preacher tells of the strange wedding gift he and his bride received at their wedding. The gift was a box marked "Yardley's After-shave Lotion." They wrote a note of thanks to the giver for the lotion. Months later they opened the shaving lotion box only to find, to their embarrassment, a very attractive cut glass vase. They had in their possession a very valuable gift but were unaware of its value for it had never been unwrapped.

A lot of believers have treated spiritual gifts in a similar way. It's time to unwrap them, and that's what we'll do in the next three chapters.

Frank M. Boyd states, "Unless the gifts of the Spirit are clearly defined and carefully classified in the first place, their purpose will not be apprehended; they may be misused; the Lord may be robbed of His glory; and the Church may fail to receive the great benefits these gifts are designed to bestow."

SENSE AND NONSENSE

Through the years, a great deal of nonsense has developed as gospel truth concerning spiritual gifts. The first error is to believe that the gifts were meant only for the Apostolic Age. Those who believe this theory tell us that supernatural signs and gifts were given to attest to the deity of Jesus, and to authenticate the first preachers of the gospel and their message.

They also argue that the necessity for such supernatural manifestations was removed upon the completion of the canon of Scripture.

This has been the stance of many non-Pentecostal evangelicals in the earlier decades of this century, but the numerous evidences of spiritual renewal in out time have caused a change of mind in many. While these friends may not accept the Pentecostal position with respect to the initial, physical evidence of the baptism in the Holy Spirit, many agree that the Pentecostals are right when they say that the gifts are still present.

There is no indication whatever in the New Testament that the gifts were meant only for the apostolic days. The way the Epistles treat the matter, only one conclusion is possible—the gifts are for the entire Church Age. The oft-quoted passage "tongues . . . shall cease" (1 Corinthians 13:8) hinges on verse 10, "when that which is perfect is come"—and that day has not yet arrived. Throughout church history there are many evidences of the manifestations of the gifts of the Spirit. To ignore the gifts is to slight the Giver!

NATURAL OR SUPERNATURAL

Another bit of nonsense is to equate the gifts of the Spirit with natural abilities. In other words, God has gifted certain men with special skills. To illustrate, the person who has unusual linguistic ability has the gift of tongues; one who has the skilled hands and abilities of the surgeon has a gift of healing.

The Scriptures clearly refute this fallacy. The gift of healing has nothing to do with medicine or surgery; prophecy is not mere preaching; speaking with tongues is not the learning of languages; nor is the word of wisdom glorified common sense. These gifts are divine endowments of the Holy Spirit. They are spiritual in essence for they spring from the Spirit. They are spiritual in expression for they are supernatural. They are spiritual in their effect for they are to edify the Church, empower the Christian, and exalt Christ. A supernatural element is introduced into Christian work and worship in addition to consecrated natural gifts.

ARE YOU WORTHY?

A third fallacy is the view that the gifts are so spectacular that they are almost unattainable, and few are holy enough to earn them. But the gifts are not limited to a few who because of special dedication and holiness are qualified to attain them. The gifts are bestowed by divine grace; they are never earned. Samuel Chadwick writes:

Spiritual gifts are no proof of spirituality. The New Testament nowhere makes spiritual gifts the sign of holiness . . . the Scriptures make it plain that in a church that "came behind in no gift, waiting for the Coming of the Lord" there were carnalities. [Samuel Chadwick, The Way to Pentecost (Berne: Light and Hope Publications, 1937), p. 110.]

This does not mean that sin is defensible in one who is filled with the Holy Spirit. It is the work of the Spirit to perfect us into the image of Christ. The Holy Spirit is not given to us or manifested through us because we are holy, good, worthy, or deserving.

ORNAMENTS OR TOOLS

Still another error exists. Some adopt the tragic view that the Church can function without the gifts. They live with the assumption that these things are not for today. Or, they look on the gifts as luxuries, or as ornaments which, while wonderful to possess, are not really needed. They treat them much as a homemaker treats her choice china which is always on display but never on the table for use.

The Scriptures clearly indicate that the gifts are tools of the Spirit to enable the Church to do the Lord's work effectively. As such they are not optional. Harold Horton states:

Spiritual gifts in the possession of believers are absolutely necessary to Christ . . . They are as necessary to Him in the carrying out of His present purposes as the limbs and faculties are to the natural body. If this is not the plain meaning of this portion (1 Corinthians 12:12-21), embodied vitally as it is in this chapter dealing specifically with the gifts of the Spirit, it has no meaning at all. [Harold Horton, *The Gifts of the Spirit* (Letchworth, Herts, Great Britain: Letchworth Printer Ltd., 1934), p. 35.] (U.S. edition now published by Gospel Publishing House.)

TWO BASIC WORDS

Two basic words are used by Paul when writing about what we call spiritual gifts—*charisma* (plural charismata) and *pneumatika*. The first is used 17 times in the New Testament and with one exception (1 Peter 4:10) is exclusive to Paul (Romans 1:11; 5:15,16; 6:23; 11:29; 12:6; 1 Corinthians 1:7; 7:7; 12:4,9,28,30,31; 2 Corinthians 1:11; 1 Timothy 4:14; 2 Timothy 1:6). The word bears the meaning of "gifts of grace." It is of interest that the gifts of the Spirit go beyond the nine gifts of 1 Corinthians 12. The expanded list of Romans 12 should not be ignored.

Pneumatika is an adjective meaning "spiritual." Some translations render the opening words of 1 Corinthians 12, "Now concerning *spirituals*." Anthony D. Palma points out that both *charismata* and *pneumatika* are used in parallel statements: "Covet earnestly the best gifts [*charismata*]" (1 Corinthians

12:31), and, "Desire spiritual gifts [*pneumatika*]" (1 Corinthians 14:1). He states that the words are used interchangeably, but *charismata* emphasizes that they are *gifts* of the Spirit, whereas *pneumatika* emphasizes that they are gifts of the *Spirit*. "In other words, the gifts are neither earned nor humanly generated."

The full complement of the *spirituals* is designated as *charismata*. They are both spiritual benefits and spiritual endowments. Set in the Church by God (1 Corinthians 12:28), the gifts remain in the custody and control of the Holy Spirit. These enablements are distributed to the members "severally as he will." In other words, they reside in the Spirit and not in man; they are manifested and not imparted. The gifts are entirely independent of human abilities and totally supernatural. As such they are manifested according to the will of God and not on the basis of human merit.

FOUR KEY PASSAGES

The New Testament repeatedly speaks of the wonderful gifts of the Spirit. In the Book of Acts they are mentioned often in the description of the Church. At times the references are to the more spectacular gifts such as, speaking in tongues, the working of miracles, and healings; at other times the less discernible gifts are prominent. The author of the Epistle to the Hebrews speaks of "[our] great salvation," to which God bore "witness, both with signs and wonders, and with divers miracles, and gifts of the Holy Ghost, according to his own will" or, as the Revised Standard Version states, "distributed according to his own will (2:3,4). But no one speaks as much about the gifts as the apostle Paul.

The Biblical pattern for the gifts is given in four passages of Scripture: 1 Corinthians 12,13,14 (chapter 12 outlines the pattern, 13 shows the balance of love, and 14 deals with regulation); Romans 12:3-8; Ephesians 4:7-16; and 1 Peter 4:10,11.

Let's take a look at the list of gifts which Paul enumerates:

1 *Corinthians* 12:4-11
word of wisdom
word of knowledge
faith
gifts of healing
working of miracles
prophecy
discerning of spirits
tongues
interpretation of tongues

1 *Corinthians* 12:28-30
apostles
prophets
teachers
miracles
gifts of healings
helps
governments or administration
tongues
interpretation of tongues

Romans 12:6-8
prophecy
ministry or service
teaching
exhortation or encouragement
giving or contributing
ruling or leading
doing acts of mercy

Ephesians 4:7-12
apostles
prophets
evangelists
pastors and teachers

FOUR KEY WORDS

Four key words occur in the four key passages in 1 Corinthians, Romans, Ephesians, and 1 Peter. These words are *grace, gift, body,* and *member.* The word *grace* indicates that the gift is unmerited. It does not come as a bonus for goodness. *Gift* indicates that the manifestation finds its origin in the grace of God.

It is grace in manifestation. The word *body* shows that the gifts are for the profit of the Church, the body of Christ. The fourth key word, *member*, points to the fact that the divine empowerings operate through individual members.

FOUR KEY STATEMENTS

Paul makes four significant statements in 1 Corinthians 12:

1. There are varieties of gifts, but the same Spirit (v. 4).
2. There are differences of ministries, but the same Lord (v. 5).
3. There are diversities of operations, but the same God (v. 6).
4. There are many members, but one Body (vv. 12,14).

THREE MANIFESTATIONS

The foregoing statements in 1 Corinthians 12 indicate that there are three manifestations of the Spirit:

1. Gifts of the Spirit
2. Administrations or gifts of ministry
3. Operations of the Spirit

These are to occur in the body of Christ through the various members. The word *body* occurs 18 times in the chapter; *member*, 14 times; and *gift*, 6 times.

THERE'S A MINISTRY FOR YOU

Every member has a ministry to perform, a function to fulfill in the body of Christ. These functions are termed *ministries*. They range from the four major ministries of apostle, prophet, evangelist, and pastor-teacher (Ephesians 4:11) to those Paul names as ministry: exhortation, giving, ruling, showing mercy (Romans 12:3-8), helps, governments (1 Corinthians 12:28).

NEITHER BALLOTS NOR COMMITTEES

Who gives direction as to where the individual member will function? The Lord does. He knows if a foot, an ear, or an eye is needed (1 Corinthians 12:18-25). Effectual ministry in the Body is brought about by every member functioning as it pleases God. The gifts and the ministries are not the product of ballots and committees; they come to the Church from her living Head. He gives, the members receive. The members exercise "according to the grace that is given . . . [and] the proportion of faith" (Romans 12:6). The gifts are potentially present in every Spirit-filled Christian by the presence and power of the Holy Spirit.

THE COMMON GOOD

There was a wide variety of gifts in the Apostolic Church, but always the emphasis was on the unity of the Body (Romans 12:4-6; 1 Corinthians 12:12-27; Ephesians 4:4-16). The variety always functions within the unity of the Body. The unity is fundamental for "to each one is given the manifestation of the Spirit for the common good" (1 Corinthians 12:7, NASB).

WHAT ARE YOU TO DO?

As a Spirit-filled Christian you have a twofold responsibility. You are to find and fulfill your God-given minstry in the body of Christ, and you are to be ready at any moment for the Holy Spirit to use you in that *ministry* and by whatever *gift* He may choose.

11

Concerning Spiritual Gifts
PART 2

Twenty years separated two very similar and beautiful experiences in which I was directly involved. Both took place at the dedication services of Assemblies of God churches. The first occurred in 1949 at New Ulm, Minnesota. Following the dedication of the building erected by Herman Hagemeister there was an utterance in tongues accompanied by the interpretation. At the conclusion of the service a lady from Mankato, Minnesota came to me and said, "My father is a Jew, and I am half Jewish. That which was spoken was in perfect Yiddish. Both of us understood it." For a moment the thought flashed through my mind—"What about the interpretation? Was it correct? This is the acid test." Then she continued, "And what you said was a perfect translation."

Again the setting was similar. The new building of First Assembly in St. Louis Park, Minnesota, Edwin B. Hollen, pastor, was being dedicated in 1969. Present in the service was a Jewess and her children as guests of her maid who attended the church. Following the dedication there was an utterance in tongues with the interpretation. As the utterance in tongues was proceeding, the boy turned to his mother and said, "Mother, why are they talking in Hebrew?"

These are but two of several instances to which

I can give testimony to being present when people have been in the audience who understood the language which was spoken. More than once I have heard people magnify God or engage in prayer in one of the Scandinavian languages which I understand. They were friends whom I knew could not speak the tongue.

I was present when a Greek restaurateur came into a service in my home church. A lady spoke in tongues, but there was no interpretation. The Greek, an unsaved man, turned ashen white. The lady who spoke was his competitor three or four doors down the street. She was speaking to him about his soul's salvation in his native tongue, and he knew that she could neither speak nor understand the Greek language.

These are manifestations of two of the nine gifts of the Spirit listed in 1 Corinthians 12. They are supernatural enablements of the Holy Spirit. Let's take a closer look at them.

Generally the gifts are divided into groups of three: (1) the mind of God—the word of wisdom, the word of knowledge, discerning of spirits; (2) the power of God—faith, gifts of healing, working of miracles; (3) the voice of God—prophecy, tongues, the interpretation of tongues. Myer Pearlman calls the three groups the power to know supernaturally, to act supernaturally, to speak supernaturally. Harold Horton and Howard Carter speak of them as three gifts of revelation, three gifts of power, and three gifts of inspiration. Donald Gee divides the gifts as five gifts of utterance and four gifts of power. Anthony Palma includes discerning of spirits with prophecy, tongues, and interpretation, pointing out the close connection between prophecy and discerning of spirits.

True wisdom is God's possession and is resident in Him, infinite and limitless in measure. The Scriptures tell us that in Christ "are hid all the treasures of wisdom and knowledge" (Colossians 2:3). The word of wisdom is a portion of that infinite wisdom of God, which He chooses to reveal through a Spirit-filled believer. This enablement is not the gift of wisdom in the abstract sense, but the word of wisdom.

This word of wisdom is not diplomacy, tact, human skill, glorified intelligence, or psychology. No amount of experience develops this wisdom; it is supernatural. It is wisdom given of God through the Holy Spirit for the need of the hour. Jesus spoke of this when He said, "When they bring you unto the synagogues, and unto magistrates, and powers, take ye no thought how or what thing ye shall answer, or what ye shall say: For the Holy Ghost shall teach you in the same hour what ye ought to say . . . For I will give you a mouth and wisdom, which all your adversaries shall not be able to gainsay or resist" (Luke 12:11,12; 21:15).

In a manifestation of this gift something beyond our human wisdom flashes on. There is a sense of the divine, of the right thing being said, a direction as to the right course. The manifestation may occur in a preaching situation (1 Corinthians 2:13), in a church problem (Acts 6:1-7), or in a pressing emergency (Matthew 21:23-27; 22:17-22). As Donald Gee states, it is "a spoken utterance through a direct operation of the Holy Spirit at a given moment, rather than an abiding deposit of supernatural wisdom." An illustration of this gift is James' decision at the council in Jerusalem regarding the vexing problem of the relation of Gentile Christians to Jewish law (Acts 15:13-21).

The word of knowledge is a divine communication by revelation of facts relating to earth which are not known. As important as a knowledge of the Word of God is, this gift is not a knowledge of the Word. That knowledge comes by application to prayerful study. It's God's wireless, knowledge supernaturally imparted, a manifestation of divine omniscience. This manifestation is not by scholarly achievement; it neither makes a scholar nor can it be attained by mental acumen, education, study, or experience.

Ananias was supernaturally given needed knowledge about Saul, the great persecutor, and ministered to him (Acts 9:10-16) leading him to Christ. Peter received this word on the housetop concerning Cornelius (Acts 10). Elisha by this manifestation knew the plans of the king of Syria (2 Kings 6:8-12).

We were in a large meeting in a city auditorium. Among the many who came one night in response to the invitation was a stranger to me. Suddenly I was seized by the Spirit and charged him with being a whited sepulchre filled with vile sins beneath the veneer of refinement. The knowledge came by the Spirit; it was not by being able to judge his character and life patterns, nor by human psychology.

The man fled behind the platform and crawled into a storage area. I followed him and found him pouring out a catalog of filth to God in confession and repentance. The knowledge came to me only from God, and the Spirit used it to bring the man to salvation.

DISCERNING OF SPIRITS

This manifestation has nothing to do with ESP. Nor does this come through training, but it is given in a moment when and as it is needed. It is not by keen insight into human nature such as a psychiatrist may have. Thus it is not human shrewdness, character reading, fault finding, or thought reading. Nor is it natural discernment of humans, nor even spiritual discernment (1 Corinthians 2:14).

Rotherham speaks of it as discrimination of spirits. Alford calls it distinction of spirits—the power to distinguish between the operations of the Spirit of God, evil spirits, and the unassisted human spirit (1 John 4:1; 1 Timothy 4:1; 1 Corinthians 14:29).

The real nature of this gift is knowing and judging, but never guessing. It is to know what is in a person and to know the spirit. The Church is guarded against evil spirits and deceivers, and they are exposed.

When unspiritual or prejudiced people judge or condemn, they are not exercising this gift. A critical spirit is not spiritual.

Biblical examples of the gift are many. Peter exposed the lying of Ananias and Sapphira (Acts 5:1-11). He discerned the deceit of Simon the sorcerer (Acts 8:23). Paul discerned that Elymas was a child of the devil (Acts 13:6-12), and unmasked the demon spirit in the fortune-teller at Philippi and delivered her (Acts 16:16-18). By the Spirit Elisha perceived Gehazi's deceit (2 Kings 5:20-27) and Hazael's bloody mind (2 Kings 8:7-15).

There are also Biblical standards for "trying the spirits" (Matthew 7:15-23; 1 Corinthians 12:3; 1 John 4:1-6), and by these the claims of a gift of discerning of spirits can be accurately assessed.

FAITH

The gift of faith is not saving faith, although that, too, is a gift of God (Ephesians 2:8). J. Narver Gortner states that the gift of faith is mountain-moving faith (Mark 11:23). Faith is no kin to mortal trust; it is special faith, miraculous faith. This is not the faith by which we live; it comes in the emergency, at the moment of extreme need; it is miraculous assurance. The raising of people from the dead, such as Dorcas, undoubtedly was through the manifestation of the gift of faith and, of course, that was the working of a miracle. Faith ends and miracles and healings begin.

Jesus said, "Have the faith of God" (Mark 11:22 margin). Possibly that is the gift of faith—a measure of divine faith dropped miraculously into the heart—what great things can then be done! An example is the healing of the lame man at the gate of the temple (Acts 3:1-11,16).

GIFTS OF HEALING

There must be some significance to the fact that the word *gifts* is absent from the other eight *spirituals* and yet is attached to *healing*, or literally *healings*, and then in the plural whenever healing is mentioned. It appears to indicate that none of us can claim a gift of healing, but rather that God in His sovereignty may empower an individual with a bestowment of healings as the occasion demands to the glory of God.

Divine healing is an integral part of the gospel, provided for in the Atonement, and is the privilege of all believers. And gifts of healings are one of the manifestations of the Spirit. But just as the gift of wisdom does not make you wise, gifts of healings will not make you a healer. Like every other gift, this one rests in the sovereignty of God. This bestowment does not mean that one so used could heal all cases of sickness. Such was the case in apostolic days, and such is true today. Our place is to preach the Word and expect signs to follow. Healing was very prominent in the ministry of Jesus and the apostles and has been a vital part of the Pentecostal revival of this century.

WORKING OF MIRACLES

There are three New Testament words for miracles. The first is *dunamis* which can be translated "power"; the second is *teras* meaning "wonder"; the third is *semeion* meaning "sign." Note what Peter said of Jesus in his sermon at Pentecost: "Jesus of Nazareth, a man approved of God among you by *miracles* and *wonders* and *signs,* which God did by him in the midst of you . . ." (Acts 2:22).

In the narrowest Biblical sense, a miracle is an event occuring in the physical world which cannot be accounted for by any of its known sources. Miracles are works contrary to nature resulting from a supernatural intervention, an interruption of the system of nature as we know it. A miracle is a manifestation of supernatural power in the natural realm.

Examples are: the passage through the Red Sea (Exodus 14:13-22); the water springing out of the rock in the wilderness (Exodus 17:5-7); the lengthening of the day for Joshua (Joshua 10:12-14); the provision of oil to pay the widow's debt (2 Kings 4:1-7); the restoration of Eutychus (Acts 20:9,10); the special miracles by the hands of Paul (Acts 19:11,12). Miracles were everywhere visible in the ministry of Jesus and the apostles. And the day of miracles is not past.

DIVERS KINDS OF TONGUES

Speaking in tongues is expressing words one has never learned, but which are directly communicated by the Holy Spirit. The utterance does not come by conceptual forethought in the vocalization by the speaker. It is "as the Spirit [gives] utterance" (Acts 2:4).

"Taken alone," states D. H. McLaughlin, "the gift of tongues is for private prayer and worship (1 Corinthians 14:14,15,28). With its sister gift of interpretation, it becomes a means of edifying the church (1 Corinthians 14:5). On the Day of Pentecost it was a sign to the unbelieving who heard it. It might well still be a sign where under certain circumstances the language spoken, not understood by the speaker, may be understood by the hearers."

Tongues constitutes a vocal rather than a mental miracle. Your mind becomes a spectator, and your ears become listeners. In your personal life speaking in tongues brings rich personal edification; you are built up spiritually. In the church, with the accompanying gift of interpretation, tongues edify the church.

The gift of tongues can be public prayer (1 Corinthians 14:13-16). The interpretation can be petition, praise, or thanksgiving. The gift is not for personal guidance, nor for the spread of the gospel.

Tongues as the evidence of the baptism in the Spirit and tongues as a gift are alike in nature but diverse in purpose and use. The former is spoken by all who receive the Baptism, the latter by those who are used to exercise the gift.

INTERPRETATION OF TONGUES

A spiritual gift of great value in an assembly of believers is described as "the interpretation of tongues." As a manifestation of the Spirit, vastly superior to human thought and volition, this gift may be defined as an inspired explanation in commonly understood language of an inspired utterance in unknown tongues. As the utterance when speaking in tongues is not conceived in the mind, so the utterance of interpretation proceeds from the Spirit rather than from the intellect of the person.

The gift is one of interpretation—not translation—of tongues. It means to explain thoroughly, and as such it can be descriptive or literal. In my personal experience I have seen the gift operate in both ways, for I have understood the unknown tongue and could testify to the accuracy of the interpretation. On one occasion it was a literal translation.

D. H. McLaughlin states that " interpretations, like prophecy, should be in the third person."

PROPHECY

New Testament prophecy, which is different from ordinary preaching, is a supernatural manifestation given for edification, exhortation, and comfort. From 1 Corinthians 14:30 we learn that the gift comes by means of a revelation through the Spirit. For the most part, it is forthtelling and not foretelling but, like the sister gift of tongues, it may have the element of revelation, knowledge, or doctrine. Prophecy is unpremeditated utterance which is not preaching, although it may come out in a Spirit-filled message.

The greater part of 1 Corinthians 14 is devoted to the consideration of this gift, comparing it with the other gifts and especially with the gift of tongues. Prophecy is shown to be greater than tongues unless tongues is accompanied by interpretation (1 Corinthians 14:23-25).

12
Knowing the Regulations

Contractors and builders talk about "specs"—the specifications. Bureaucrats discuss the "regs"—the regulations that relate to policies to be followed to fulfill the laws. God has also laid down specifications and regulations. Those that pertain to the operation of the gifts of the Spirit are found in 1 Corinthians.

God's Word states, "For God hath not given us the spirit of fear; but of power, and of love, and of a sound mind" (2 Timothy 1:7). First Corinthians 12, 13, and 14 fall into a natural category of fulfilling that verse. Chapter 12 deals with the power—the mighty supernatural spirituals. Chapter 13 confines itself to the virtues and motivation of love. Chapter 14 shows the way of balance and regulation; it gives us the pattern of soundness, a sound mind.

Our ministries and our treasure are "in earthen vessels, that the excellency of the power may be of God, and not of us" (2 Corinthians 4:7). But we must remember that while these mighty bestowments are of God, they operate through human channels. And further, they are not exercised mechanically through impassive instruments; there is cooperation by the person being used.

MOTIVATION AND REGULATION

Two factors are very important if believers are

to be edified, Christ is to be glorified, and God's kingdom extended. Personal spiritual growth and effective service for God hinge on these two, namely, motivation and regulation.

The gifts of the Spirit are not given to promote human personality. With regret we acknowledge that we have seen people who have sought to advance their own popularity and increase their chances of promotion by a demonstration of a so-called gift. This was also true in apostolic times. Recall Simon the sorcerer (Acts 8) who, desiring privilege and popularity, wanted to buy the power of God. Simon has had many unworthy disciples through the centuries who, with unconcealed piety, have selfishly desired spiritual gifts to promote their own ends.

A TENTH GIFT

One lady boastfully claimed to have all nine gifts. The preacher corrected her and said, "You have a tenth, the gift of bragging."

MISPLACED HALOS

Unfortunately many people are swayed by manifestations and place a halo over those who frequently exercise the gifts. Sad to say, there are those who glory in such an image and seek to increase their spiritual status by an increase in manifestations. To all such Peter had a good word, "Why look ye so earnestly on us, as though by our own power or holiness we had made this man to walk?" (Acts 3:12).

Spirit-filled people are exposed to various dangers. After the Spirit descended upon Jesus (Matthew 3:16), He was tempted of the devil to use His power to satisfy His fleshly appetite, to put on an egocentric exhibition, and to gain the entire world without going to Golgotha (Matthew 4:1-11). In the centuries since, the devil has approached Christians in these ways by taking Scripture out of context and causing them to overemphasize some facet of divine truth at the expense of ignoring other equally important portions of Scripture.

MADNESS

The apostle Paul wrote, "If therefore the whole church be come together into one place, and all speak with tongues, and there come in those that are unlearned, or unbelievers, will they not say that ye are mad?" (1 Corinthians 14:23).

MADNESS . . . RIGHT AND WRONG

There is a madness which is of faith and a madness which is of fanaticism. The former is manifested by an utter devotion to God and His holy will (Mark 3:21; Acts 26:24). The latter is something which has plagued Christianity since the apostolic days. The fear of the latter must never be allowed to drive us from practicing the former.

CURE FOR FANATICISM

Fanaticism has only one simple cure, the plain, practical teaching of the Word of God. John Wesley said, "Try all things by the written Word, and let all things bow down to it. You are in danger of enthusiasm [which meant fanaticism in the eighteenth century] every hour if you depart ever so little from Scripture; yea, or from the plain, literal meaning of any text, taken in connection with the context." To which the prophet Isaiah gives witness: "To the law and to the testimony: if they speak not according to this word, it is because there is no light in them" (Isaiah 8:20).

The Holy Spirit who inspired and authored the Word honors its laws and operates within its boundaries. He says, "In each of us the Spirit is manifested in one particular way, for some useful purpose (1 Corinthians 12:7, NEB).

TOOLS, NOT TOYS

Spiritual gifts are not toys with which to play; they are tools of the Spirit to do God's work effectively. When spiritual manifestations are scripturally patterned, they fulfill the need for supernatural ministry in and to the body of Christ.

"Desire spiritual gifts" (1 Corinthians 14:1) is as much of an authoritative injunction as "Let all things be done decently and in order" (v. 40). The admitted abuse of the spiritual gifts in the Corinthian church gave no license to bar their manifestation.

The Corinthians needed instruction in many things. Unholy strife and emulation was present. Apparently undue value was placed upon speaking with tongues because of its spectacular nature. Whereas in Corinth the main difficulty had to do with tongues, it had to do with prophecy in the Thessalonian church (1 Thessalonians 5:20; 2 Thessalonians 2:2). To the latter comes the clear word, "Despise not prophesyings." Neither abuses nor excesses serve as reasons to suppress the gifts.

A MASTERLY EXAMPLE

Note how Paul deals with the problem in Corinth. He takes cognizance of their ignorance as being the underlying cause of their disorder (1 Corinthians 12: 1). He proceeds to lay a groundwork of teaching to establish the doctrinal basis as to the diversity and distribution of the gifts. "There are diversities of gifts, but the same Spirit . . . differences of administrations, but the same Lord . . . diversities of operations, but it is the same God" (vv. 4-6).

Paul proceeds in chapter 13 with another and most

important phase—motivation. Notice his boldness, "Though I speak . . . though I have . . . though I bestow . . . and have not love, I am nothing. . . ." Their childish misconceptions (v. 11) had given them an inverted sense of values.

The remarkable skill and wisdom used by Paul in becoming both corrective and instructive in chapter 14 is to be coveted. Negative correction is based on positive teaching. Improper practice is remedied by directing their zeal. Their understanding is changed by building them up in truth. While abuses are being corrected, the Corinthians are urged to "desire . . . covet . . . covet earnestly . . . seek [to] excel to the edifying of the church." With the heart of a true pastor, Paul knew that the important food for his flock was the truth of the Word.

MATURITY

First, Paul calls for mature understanding: "Brethren, be not children in understanding: howbeit in malice be ye children, but in understanding be men" (v. 20). It's a sign of immaturity for you to close your mind to truth.

EDIFICATION

Second, he calls for the need for edification of the Church (v. 26). Edification is referred to seven times (vv. 3,4,5,12,17,26). Edification means building up, adding, or contributing to others. Often in Scripture, the blending together of people in spiritual worship is likened to erecting a building—a spiritual habitation (1 Peter 2:5). Many lack the insight to distinguish between their own desire to speak in tongues and the moving of the Spirit upon them for the edification of the Church. Of the nine gifts, this is the only one of which it is said that its use is edifying to the one manifesting the gift.

Third, Paul calls for order. "For God is not the author of confusion, but of peace . . . Let all things be done decently and in order" (vv. 33,40). The Spirit who brooded over chaos and wrought order out of confusion (Genesis 1:2,3) always brings order, for God is a God of order. First Corinthians 14:23 pictures a meeting with spiritual manifestations but lacking regulation. Verse 24 pictures the benefit of regulation.

Chapter 12 develops the theme of interrelatedness among members of the Body. We need one another and must learn to value one another. Chapter 13 analyzes the core: without love at the center, all else is nothing. Chapter 14 sets the "regs" for the laws of edification.

Whatever adds to the building is in order. Whatever manifestation detracts from building the spiritual temple is out of order. Quickly we add that imperfection or abuses in the exercise of the gifts do not necessarily mean that the gifts are not genuine. God's children are at various stages of development and spiritual understanding. Genuine gifts can be wrongly used because of the imperfections of the believer.

TRAFFIC SIGNALS

Paul was used to install traffic signals to allow for orderly procedure. Unless the signals are obeyed, confusion reigns. Order requires cooperation on the part of all.

Paul teaches that the "spirits of the prophets are subject to the prophets" (v. 32). Herein lies one of the great differences between Holy Spirit possession and demon possession. Demon possession controls. The Holy Spirit also controls but only operates through willing and intelligent cooperation.

If those who exercise the gifts are unable to exercise control, then why would Scripture give the regulations of verses 19,26,27,28,30, and 32? God surely would never lay down regulations for order and then move upon His people to disobey those regulations. The Holy Spirit never makes any mistakes, but our own spirits may. Never must we allow a selfish, yes, even a proud spirit—one that is not subject to Scripture and government—to possess us. The spirit of love and the desire to glorify God and edify His Church must always motivate us.

All inspired utterance in a public meeting must be understandable. In other words, tongues require interpretation to bring profit to the listeners. The burden of the interpretation is the responsibility of the one giving the utterance in tongues. He can't speak in tongues and then feel free of responsibility. He is responsible for the interpretation if no one else interprets (v. 13).

A CALL FOR BALANCE

Speaking in tongues is not to be forbidden (v. 39), but there is need of balance. If no interpreter is present, the speaker is to remain silent and "speak to himself, and to God" (v. 28). Further, tongues and interpretations are limited to "two, or at the most by three" (v. 27). This is also true concerning prophetic utterances (v. 29).

THE WORD HAS PRIORITY

When God's servant is ministering the Word under the anointing of the Spirit, it is not very probable that the Spirit will direct another to interrupt the flow of the message through the exercise of an utterance gift. Here is where any who feel so disposed should exercise control. God used the preaching of the Word to bring the thousands to repentance and faith in Christ on the Day of Pentecost.

114

Appropriateness, consideration for others, and timing are guiding principles laid down by Paul. Balance is found in the beautiful blending of the activity of the Spirit with the regulatory activity of the Word.

FURTHER GUIDELINES

It is important to note that the New Testament Church did not depend on the gifts of inspired utterance for matters dealing with church government Acts 6:1-7 cf. 1 Timothy 3:1-13). Neither was doctrine determined by a manifestation of these gifts (Acts 15); nor are the utterance gifts to be used for the interpretation of the Scriptures, for the utterances of the prophets are themselves to be judged (1 Corinthians 14:29). Guidance does not come through the prophetic gift. It may be a confirmation of God's callings (Galatians 2:1,2).

REMEMBER AND NEVER FORGET IT

Since you are a part of the body of Christ, you are interdependent with other parts of that Body. Love and consideration should be the motives that guide your behavior. Membership in Christ's body calls for obedience to authority (1 Corinthians 12:12-30). The Spirit-filled life does not lead you to independence; you are always to be under the spiritual leadership and teaching ministry of the Church (Ephesians 4:11-16). Spiritual manifestations are always to be judged by the Word of God.

The beauty and purity of the gifts will not be maintained by quenching them. Neither are they to be limited to a favored few; monopoly is never good. One person should never be regarded as the sole voice of the Church. The manifestation of the Spirit throughout the Body is to be encouraged.

PREACHING IS CENTRAL

A gospel service should center in the preaching of the Word. Does this mean that there should not be audience participation? No! All that Paul pleaded for was balance. Too many churches today need to be stirred until there is greater participation by the members.

ANSWER TO DISORDER

Paul's answer to disorder was not formality but teaching. The Church does not need the order of a graveyard. Freedom, variety, and joyfulness are necessary. We covet spontaneous worship and those times when the Spirit moves in great swells of power.

COVET EARNESTLY

Desire for spiritual gifts is in reality a longing for the spiritual equipment necessary for the Church to fulfill its mission on earth. We are to "covet earnestly the best gifts." But what is the best gift?

The best gift is the one that is needed at the moment. The demon-possessed man didn't need to see the water turned to wine. The blind man didn't need to see the stilling of the storm on Galilee. Dead Lazarus didn't need a discourse on philosophy.

Let the Spirit work in and through us, using His gifts as the need demands. Our job is to exercise the proportion of faith.

13
The Holy Spirit Working

Who is there who has not seen a sign along a street or highway warning travelers to exercise care, with the words, CAUTION—MEN WORKING?

The Bible gives us a caution sign with regard to the workings of the Holy Spirit. We are to respect and honor His person and work. We are informed and instructed concerning His gifts and the regulations relating to their manifestation. The Bible further admonishes us with caution signals concerning our treatment of the Spirit.

On the very first page of the Old Testament we read, "The Spirit of God moved upon the face of the waters" (Genesis 1:2). And on the very last page of the Bible we find, "The Spirit and the bride say, Come" (Revelation 22:17). Between these two references there is the progressive unfolding of the person and work of the Holy Spirit. He is important!

GUILTY OF OFFENSES

Today, however, as in Paul's day, people are guilty of offenses against the Holy Spirit; believers as well as unbelievers are offenders.

SIX IN NUMBER

Relatively few Scriptures deal with sinning against the Holy Spirit; they are six in number. One, *blas-*

phemy against the Holy Spirit, is identified in the Gospels (Matthew 12:24-32; Mark 3:22-30; Luke 11:14-20). Two are found in Acts—*lying* to the Spirit (5:3,4) and *resisting* the Spirit (7:51). Three are mentioned in the Epistles—*grieving* (Ephesians 4:30), *quenching* (1 Thessalonians 5:19), and *insulting* or doing despite to the Holy Spirit (Hebrews 10:29).

Three of the admonitions of Scripture regarding the attitude of people toward the Holy Spirit relate to the unbeliever—*blaspheming, resisting,* and *insulting.* The other three—*lying to, grieving,* and *quenching*—relate to the believer. To commit any of these sins is to sin against God. All are serious offenses, but to blaspheme the Holy Spirit is spiritual suicide.

Blasphemy can never be forgiven (Mark 3:29). To *resist* the Spirit is to risk eternal loss. Those who despised Moses' law died without mercy, but a "much sorer punishment" awaits those who have "done *despite* unto the Spirit of grace" (Hebrews 10:29). Ananias and Sapphira paid an awful price for *lying* to the Spirit (Acts 5:1-10). To be guilty of *grieving* or *quenching* the Spirit can readily rob the believer of his joy and victory and even his salvation.

WITH . . . IN . . . UPON

The Holy Spirit ministers to us as human beings in three ways—*with, in,* and *upon.* He deals *with* the unregenerate to convict them of sin and to draw them to Christ. When they let slip or turn away from the Spirit's wooings they *resist* Him. Others go beyond this to *insult* or to do despite unto the Spirit of grace. Still others go to the extreme and *blaspheme.*

The Spirit is *in* believers. We become the temples of God, and the Spirit works in us to sanctify us, to make us like unto Christ. By certain attitudes and actions we *grieve* the Spirit. Some may even *lie* to Him.

118

The Spirit comes *upon* believers to equip us with power for witnessing and ministry. Care must be exercised that we do not become guilty of *quenching* the Spirit's work in and through us.

WHAT IS THE UNPARDONABLE SIN?

A lady shared her problem. While worshiping God, she would be troubled with vile and blasphemous thoughts. To her knowledge her life was free from sin otherwise, and she loved God. Finally she came to the conclusion that she had committed the unpardonable sin. Had she done so? What is the unpardonable sin?

The Bible states that all sins can be forgiven except the sin of blasphemy against the Holy Spirit (Matthew 12:24-32; Mark 3:22-30; Luke 11:14-20).

It's an appalling thought that we can so sin that we shall never have forgiveness in this life or the one to come. Cases are on record where those harassed by the thought that they had committed this sin have attempted suicide or have needed to be confined to a hospital for the insane.

NOT DONE IN IGNORANCE

To find out what this sin is, let's first ascertain what it is not.

The unpardonable sin is not sin that is done in ignorance. Paul writes of himself, "Who was before a blasphemer . . . but I obtained mercy, because I did it ignorantly in unbelief (1 Timothy 1:13).

Neither is the sin of resisting the Holy Spirit unpardonable. Paul was among the number who were charged with that guilt as Stephen was martyred, and Paul later became a believer (Acts 7:51).

What then is the sin which is beyond pardon?

All blasphemy against the Holy Spirit is sin; but all sin against the Spirit is not blasphemy. Provision is made for every sin, no matter how vile, at Calvary. There is even provision for blasphemy against the Saviour (Matthew 12:32), and all offenses against the Holy Spirit can be repented of and forgiven, except blasphemy. This is borne out in 1 John 5:16,17, "There is a sin unto death: I do not say that he shall pray for it. All unrighteousness is sin: and there is a sin not unto death."

BLASPHEMY IS . . .

Blasphemy is the "expression of contempt for the personality and authority of deity, and grossly unworthy conduct in the face of the divine," states L. Thomas Holdcroft.

The sin of blasphemy against the Spirit is not unpardonable because of some arbitrary decree of God, for God is eternally a God of infinite mercy and grace (2 Peter 3:9; Matthew 11:28). In other words, the unavailability of forgiveness is not because of a lack in Christ's provision at Calvary, nor a lack in God's ability to extend grace, nor His unwillingness to pardon. Rather, it rests in the fact that the sin itself makes pardon impossible.

The sin of unbelief brings the wrath of God upon us. As long as we continue in unbelief, we are unsaved and under condemnation (John 3:36). But unbelief is not an *act* of sin for which there is no forgiveness.

THE SPIRIT WORKS

Your salvation is the result of the work of the Trinity. The Father planned it, the Son provided it, and the Holy Spirit brings it about. The work of the Father and the Son is completed. The Holy Spirit as the divine Administrator has a continuing work until the saved are gathered home at Christ's coming to receive His Church.

The Holy Spirit conveys the benefits of Calvary to us. He presents the good tidings of salvation, convicts us of sin, and enables repentance and faith. The Spirit is the lifeline between God and us. Our only way through Christ to the Father is by the Holy Spirit. He convicts, draws, woos, and makes our hearts responsive to the preaching of the gospel. No man can even say with a true confession that Jesus is Lord except by the Holy Spirit (1 Corinthians 12:3). Since the Spirit is the One who implants the life of the Saviour in us, rejection of the Spirit is rejection of that life. To reject and despise the Spirit is to reject God's only means of His grace to us.

What Jesus was speaking of was not one isolated act, but a planned course of continuing action which culminates in a condition which places a person irrevocably outside God's ability to forgive.

This act of spiritual suicide is not the result of God's anger, nor of His refusal to forgive; the act is such that God is in a position where He cannot forgive. This spiritual suicide is the result of malicious perversion and persistent opposition to the known truth of God's acts of mercy and grace, doing so with conscious deliberation and without compunction, remorse, or shame. The person who follows this course is utterly impenitent.

To ascribe the works of the Spirit to the devil and demon power cuts the lifeline, for the Spirit alone can bridge the gulf of unbelief. To be guilty of the ultimate guilt of blasphemy is to be guilty of "an eternal sin" (Mark 3:29, NASB).

INSULTING THE SPIRIT

In Hebrews 10:29 we read of those who trod "under foot the Son of God, and [count] the blood of the covenant . . . an unholy thing, and [do] despite unto the Spirit of grace." In 20th-century language, to do *despite* is to *insult* and *outrage* the Holy Spirit who imparts grace (see the Amplified Translation). To treat His offers of grace with scorn and contempt is to insult the Spirit.

RESISTING THE SPIRIT

A third attitude toward the Holy Spirit is to *resist* Him. This involves the mystery of conscience which is God's, and God's voice. To resist the claims of Christ as Saviour is to resist the Spirit. The emphasis is upon a stubborn, hard rejection of the Lord's work of regeneration. When Stephen leveled his bombshell before the council, "Ye stiffnecked and uncircumcised in heart and ears, ye do always resist the Holy Ghost" (Acts 7:51), he was condemning their willfulness and perversity.

GRIEVING THE SPIRIT

The Holy Spirit is very sensitive. He is easily grieved—so easily, in fact, that you can be guilty of having done so while hardly being aware of it. It's important that you are aware of those things that grieve this wonderful Heavenly Dove, the Comforter and Helper of the Trinity.

"Grieve not the holy Spirit of God" (Ephesians 4: 30) is a very definite command of Scripture. I believe that none of us as Christians really wants to grieve Him. How can we avoid doing so?

ASSOCIATED WITH LOVE

To *grieve*, the dictionary tells us, means to "cause pain of mind; to injure; to harm; to occasion grief to; to try" someone. The root meaning of the word is "to make sorrowful." Further, *grieve* is a word associated only with love. We can't grieve one who doesn't love us. We may annoy, hurt, or anger such a person, but we can't grieve him.

Only a disciple, Judas, could betray Jesus; not an enemy. Others could wrong Him, persecute Him, do despite to Him; but only a friend could grieve Him.

A good mother never hates her child, no matter what the child does; but she is deeply grieved over that child's misdeeds and sins. Whenever our thoughts, our words, our deeds, our attitudes are unworthy of our Christian profession, the Holy Spirit is grieved.

SINS WHICH GRIEVE

Let's look more closely at the offenses which cause the Spirit to grieve as they are listed in the Ephesians context. They are summarized under three headings: (1) sins of speech; (2) sins of attitude; (3) sins of action.

Sins of *speech* are defined as the "former conversation" (Ephesians 4:22), lying (4:25), corrupt communication (4:29), evil speaking (4:31), filthy and foolish talking (5:4). We are to speak the truth in love, for the Holy Spirit who abides within is the Spirit of Truth. There is no place for us to use shady stories, questionable jokes, foul language, gossip, talebearing, and the like. To do so is to grieve the Spirit.

Sins of *attitude* include bitterness (long-standing resentment), wrath (impulsive anger), anger (habitual temper), clamor (argumentative, divisive, troublemaking spirit), malice (ill will, grudge) (Ephesians 4:31). Greed, covetousness, and selfishness (5:3) are also in this list of sins which bring pain to the Spirit.

Sins of *action* are all "unfruitful works of darkness" (Ephesians 5:11). Some specific sins are stealing (4:28) which includes robbing God of His tithes, sexual immorality (5:3), drunkenness (5:18). Persist in these things, and not only do you grieve the Spirit, but you can grieve Him away. We must make no place for living after the flesh. "Do not participate in the unfruitful deeds of darkness, but instead even expose them" (Ephesians 5:11, NASB).

QUENCHING THE SPIRIT

Among several terse reminders in 1 Thessalonians 5 is the command, "*Quench* not the Spirit" (v. 19). The Holy Spirit comes *upon* the believer in baptizing power. To *quench* means "to suppress, to stifle, to put out the fire." The translation by Phillips reads, "Never damp the fire of the Spirit," and that by Williams, "Stop stifling the Spirit." The marginal note states that this is a "figure of putting out fire by smothering."

The following verse in Thessalonians is, "*Despise* not prophesyings (v. 20). The idea of the word *despise* is to "treat with contempt." True, we are to "prove all things [and] hold fast that which is good" (v. 21), but there is no place for us to have a harsh, critical spirit. Through that kind of a spirit we throw cold water on the Spirit. Neither are we to suppress the promptings of the Spirit to manifest a gift, providing there is a proper scriptural setting. Interestingly, the verb translated *quench* appears in the words of the foolish virgins who said, "Our lamps are going out" (Matthew 25:8, NASB).

LYING TO THE SPIRIT

Because He is the *Holy Spirit*, deception and falsehood are repulsive to Him. Ananias sought spiritual status and prestige by lying. Peter exploded his hypocrisy and said, "Why hath Satan filled thine heart to lie to the Holy Ghost?" (Acts 5:3). Judgment came, and it exemplifies that which will eventually happen to all who commit this offense unless they repent. They may not drop dead at the time they commit the sin, but they will face it at the judgment.

Every helpful act of the Holy Spirit toward saint or sinner is an act of grace. Mercy, grace, blessing, and cleansing bring responsibility, and responsibility ultimately leads to accountability (Romans 14:12).

How alert we should be to the presence of the Spirit; how we need to tune the inner ear to His gentle voice. Beware lest we create an unwelcome climate or hostile atmosphere for His presence. Like Samson, we can be unaware of losing the presence of God (Judges 16:20).

He who was the creating Force of the universe is as gentle as a dove, and like a sensitive dove He can be frightened away. Never let your human will, your organized program, or your earthly plan supplant His leadership. Guard against the unkind word, the wrong attitude, the unchristlike act which will hinder His presence and work.

Paul used several negatives to call our attention to the positive. Note them again: "Grieve [translated vex in Isaiah 63:10] not . . . Quench not . . . Despise not . . . Forbid not." He states further, "Prove all things; hold fast that which is good" (1 Thessalonians 5:21). You and I are called to patience and scriptural steadfastness—to wait, to listen, and to learn.

CAUTION . . . THE HOLY SPIRIT IS WORKING!

The H. S.
1. enriches study life Jn. 16:13
2. enriches prayer life Rom. 8:26
                            Jude 20
3. enriches emotional life Rom 14:17
We are to be filled in order for
him to do His work thru us.

Come H.S I need thee
" sweet S I pray
" in thy strength & thy power
" in thine own gentle way.

Gifts - total of 22 gifts   Gifts of Sp.
Revelation - Wisdom   non-
              Knowledge   resident
              Discerning

Power - Healing
        Faith
        Miracles

Utterance - tongues
          - interpretation
            prophesy.

Wisdom - supernatural revelation
         of divine purpose
Knowledge - supernatural rev. of
            facts in God's mind

Eph 4.